BLOOD BROTHERS

Best Wishes,

PHILIP G. SAMAAN

Collegedale, Tennessee 37315

Reedited by Dr. Philip G. Samaan
Designed by Dennis Ferree
Cover art and cover design by Frank Strack
Typeset in 11/13 Garamond

The author assumes full responsibility for the accuracy of all
facts and quotations cited in this book.

Unless otherwise indicated, Scripture references in this book
are from the New King James Version.

ISBN 0-8163-1042-4

Contents

Dedication

To my beloved father and mother, who taught me what it means
to be a true son of Abraham.

Introduction

The thundering howl of Israeli jet fighters shattered the peaceful blue sky of Beirut, roaring on their way to strike Syrian forces to the East. That was my rude introduction to the seemingly never-ending conflict between Israel and its Arab neighbors. This occured at the height of the six-day war in June of 1967 while attending a boarding school situated in the gorgeous hills overlooking the azure waters of the Mediterranean. What a contrast! Nature was all peace, but man was at war. That was the first time I witnessed one of the too many such conflicts in the region. How paradoxical it is that this special part of the world which God intended to be the fountain of peace becomes the epitome of war. How ironic it is that this cradle of civilazation should degenerate into its demise. And how tragic it is that this birthplace of the three great monotheistic religions of the world deteriorate into the very antethesis of God's paragon of love and brotherhood.

The adherents of these three monotheistic religions of Judaism, Christianity, and Islam profess to be the children of one father, Abraham, worshiping the same God of the Bible. Through Abraham, the father of many nations, the Jews trace their lineage back to Isaac, the Muslims connect their ancestry with Ishmael, and the Christians link their spiritual heritage and destiny to Christ, the true Seed of Abraham. Why then are these great peoples who have the same father and heritage, and worship the same God have such continuous conflicts?

The history of these conflicts is by no means limited to the relatively recent wars of 1948, 1956, 1967, 1973, 1982, and the countless other clashes in between. Indeed, the history spans the long annals of persecution and violence during the Dark Ages, the Crusades, the genocides of the pogroms, the massacre of the Armenians, and the Holocaust. One glaring manifestation of these atrocities occurred in September of 1982, when the children of Abraham—Jews, Christians, and Muslims—were all tragically involved. Humanity shuddered and was horrified when Christian militiamen massacred more than 800 Muslim Palestinians in the Sabra and Shatila refugee camps in Beirut under the watchful eye and passive acquiescence of the invading Israeli army.

William Johnsson describes that tragic massacre, which involved, in one way or the other, the different descendants of Abraham, all claiming to believe in the same God. Most of those massacred were grandparents, mothers, children, and babies. This time the relatives who died were Muslims, the relatives who killed them were Christians, and the other relatives who callously heard the screams were the Jewish soldiers ("Killing for God's Sake," *Liberty* [May/June 1983], pp. 2-5).

Of course, the Christians justified their actions as retaliatory measures (translated *revenge*) against other atrocities they claimed were committed against them by the Palestinian Muslims. And the feud goes on in an ever-enlarging vicious circle. Mark Twain depicts a conversation between two of his characters, Huck and Buck. "What's a feud?" "Why, where were you raised? Don't you know what a feud is?" "Never heard of it before—tell me about it." "Well," says Buck, "a feud is this way: A man has a quarrel with another man, and kills *him;* then that other man's brother kills *him;* then the other brothers, on both sides, goes for one another; then the *cousins* chip in—and by and by everybody's killed off, and there ain't no more feud. But it's kind of slow, and takes a long time" (Mark Twain, *The Adventures of Huckleberry Finn,* cited in Friedman, *From Beirut to Jerusalem,* p. vii).

To a certain degree, this blood feud among the children of Abraham can be traced all the way back to the very home of Abraham. Undoubtedly, you are familiar with the envy and strife that resulted from Sarah's insistence that Abraham marry Hagar, her Egyptian maid. They ventured to fulfill God's promise in their own human effort, in their own time and way. From the reading of the account in Genesis, it is clear that the seeds of this continual conflict were planted right there in the heart of Abraham's home. Ishmael served as proof that Abraham and Sarah planned for him to be the son of promise. That was the only reason why Abraham accepted taking Hagar as the second wife. Later, when Isaac was born, they also knew that he was the son of promise.

It was never Hagar's idea to marry her master Abraham and give him the promised son. She was simply a dutiful maid who obediently complied with the wishes of her master and mistress. Consequently, we end up with two "promised" sons vying for the attention, inheritance, and blessings of their father. God, trying to make the most out of this difficult situation, sympathized with Ishmael, richly blessed him, and made him into a great nation.

Moreover, we must not mistakenly believe that strife takes place only between Jews, Christians, and Arabs; it also occurs within those groups themselves. For example, Israel's internal politics seems often to be in a state of disunity and conflict—with the Likud and Labor parties and other factions vying for control. The inquisitions and wars in Christian Europe spanned hundreds of years, and violence continues today between Catholics and Protestants in Northern Ireland. Tribal wars existed among the ancient Arabs, and political conflicts among Muslim countries remain to this day.

The sudden and brutal Iraqi invasion of Kuwait is a striking case in point. Ongoing tensions in the Persian Gulf region continue to rivet the attention of the world on the Middle East and threaten to destabilize the entire area. Who knows what future crisis will be thrown in the face of a world that seems to be enjoying unprecedented cooperation between East and West.

The terrible civil war that began in 1975 tore Lebanon apart and showed that such tragic war was not confined to Christian and Muslim factions fighting each other. Incredibly complex and confusing, it is difficult to understand how loyalties and alliances can shift from day to day. One's loyal friend today might be one's bitter enemy tomorrow. Muslim factions fought each other to the bitter end for dominance, and competing Christian militias annihilated one another in a bid for control.

Peace and brotherhood among the nations of the Near East is not going to happen as a result of political alliances and human devising. The only hope for the descendants of Abraham is found in the true Seed of Abraham, Jesus Christ. Military campaigns and international efforts have repeatedly tried to promote peace and security in the Holy Lands, but to no avail. Albert Einstein, himself of Jewish heritage, was possibly the greatest scientist of all time. He had a deep compassion for all oppressed people everywhere. When he saw the turmoil in Palestine he moved to say that "Peace in Palestine cannot be achieved by force, but only through understanding" (Cited by Alfred Lilienthal, *The Zionist Connection—What Price Peace?* p. iii).

This book seeks to help the reader understand the spiritual significance and implications of the seed of Abraham. No attempt will be made to condone or condemn any side in this "family feud." We will, however, endeavor to walk on some common, and yet sometimes difficult and perplexing, ground that the children of Abraham share, rather than march into their battlegrounds. Indeed, through the Messiah, the Son of promise, Abraham becomes "the father of all them that believe" (Rom. 4:11).

CHAPTER
1

The Father of Faith

Members of a Palestinian Arab family were having a difficult time trying to persuade the Israelis to allow them to visit the grave of their deceased father. During the Six-Day War of 1967, their property was occupied when Israel completed its military victory over its Arab neighbors. Now the family's ancestral land had new Israeli owners. Understandably, the Israelis did not feel comfortable allowing such visitation rights to the grave site of this Arab patriarch. Long years of mutual distrust and hostility made this potentially healing human interaction among the contemporary children of Abraham seem so unlikely.

More than 3,800 years earlier, another burial site held the remains of a great patriarch in the same land of Canaan, in the cave of Machpelah by Mamre (see Genesis 25:9). There, by their deceased father Abraham, Isaac and his brother Ishmael, the progenitors of the Jews and the Arabs, stood together, reconciled by his magnanimous character and great faith in God. Years earlier, the jealousy and contention that erupted in their household had compelled their father reluctantly to oust Ishmael twice. He was ousted while his mother Hagar was still carrying him in her womb. Fourteen years later, he and his mother were again sent packing into the wilderness.

Obviously, Ishmael could have remained embittered for life against his younger brother Isaac. He was much older, and had been told by his parents that he was to be the son of promise. "Ishmael, now a youth, had been regarded by all in the encampment as the heir of Abraham's wealth and the inheritor of the blessings promised to his descendants" (*Patriarchs and Prophets*, p. 146). Moreover, his life was twice imperiled in the harsh wilderness, only to be rescued by the angel. When he was cast away as a teenager, he had to leave his father Abraham, who greatly loved and cherished him, never to see him again.

Abraham's intimate friendship with God, manifested in his stalwart faith and steadfast love, made a lasting impact on these two brothers that was to dissipate any lingering animosity. God Himself testified that Abraham was committed to training his children and household in the ways of righteousness and justice (see Genesis 18:19).

This spiritual nurture and training embraced not only Sarah, Hagar, Ishmael, his eldest servant Eliezer, and later on his second son Isaac, but also everyone connected in some way with his household or encampment. Even though Ishmael was quite likely hurt and disgruntled, and may have held some grudges, he could not rid himself of his father's spiritual upbringing. We are told that "in his latter days [Ishmael] repented of his evil ways and returned to his father's God" (ibid., p. 174). And although he was painfully cast away from his beloved father and home, he "seems to have maintained good relations with his relatives in Palestine" (*SDA Bible Dictionary*, p. 533).

Considering the present turmoil in the Holy Land among the modern descendants of Abraham, only his faith and benevolence can bring about healing and restoration. Despite all its sophisticated technology, its deft diplomacy, and its expertise in international relations, the modern world finds itself unsuccessful in wiping out the dark stains of hostility nursed by long centuries of mutual jealousy and suspicion. The only real solution is found in emulating the example of Abraham and his two sons. If this wonderful spirit of their father was capable of achieving reconciliation between them then, why not their present-day descendants?

During the Christmas season some years back, a large group of peace demonstrators composed of Jews, Christians, and Muslims—the modern sons and daughters of Abraham—formed an impressive human chain around Jerusalem. They demonstrated for peaceful negotiations, and for resolution of the political turmoil by linking themselves hand in hand in a continuous and ever-widening circle around the city of peace. The timing was ideal. This special occasion commemorated the birth of the Prince of Peace, the Seed of Abraham, who came to this troubled world to bring peace to our earth, and good will to all people (Luke 2:14).

Unfortunately, because of political and security considerations, the Israeli authorities violently dispersed this human chain of peace and unity with tear gas, water cannons, and rubber bullets, wounding about sixty of these demonstrators. Though most people want to live in peace with their families and friends, politcal leaders and governments often seem to get in the way of peaceful resolutions to conflicts.

The Koran, the holy book of the Muslims, admonishes the believers to pattern their lives after the example of Abraham. It refers to him as a model in devotion, faith, and obedience. "Abraham was indeed a model, devoutly obedient to God, (and) true in faith, and he joined not gods with God. . . . Follow the way of Abraham the true in faith" (The Holy Koran 16:120, 123). It is the incessant work of Satan, who has always been the source of all mistrust and hatred, to divide and conquer God's children, even members of the same family. The Koran again beckons the Jews, the Christians, and the Muslims, the descendants of father Abraham, to come together around the common truth of loyalty to one heritage and one God (Koran 2:62).

Who was this Abraham, and how did he become our model of faith in God and friendship with Him? In considering all the people of the world at that time, why did God choose this one man for the glorious purpose of blessing many nations and bringing His salvation to them? The divine election of Abraham is not merely an affirmation of him, but, more important, a commentary on God's magnificent character.

Even the change of his name from Abram to Abraham reveals that his divine mission was not to be limited to just a family, a tribe, or a nation, but it was to be universal, encompassing the many multitudes of the earth. The name Abram means "the exalted father," and the name Abraham refers to "the father of a multitude." And a "multitude" in the context of Genesis 17:4-6 points clearly not only to one nation, the nation of Israel, but to many nations. "No longer shall your name be called Abram, but your name shall be Abraham; for I have made you a father of many nations" (verse 5). In fact, when God initially called Abraham to leave his home in Ur of the Chaldees, He promised that through him not only many nations will be blessed, but that "*all* the families of the *earth* shall be blessed" (Genesis 12:3, emphasis supplied).

Abraham was born in approximately 1950 B.C. in Ur of the Chaldees as the youngest son in the household of Terah his father. He was the ninth generation descended from Shem, the eldest son of Noah. And through this unbroken line of Shem, Noah, Methuselah, Enoch, Seth, and Adam, God meticulously safe guarded a faithful remnant to maintain the shining light of His truth in the midst of moral darkness.

Even in his own home, young Abraham was not shielded from idolatry. His relatives, even his own father Terah, mixed the worship of God with devotion to other heathen deities. Joshua reminded the children of Israel of this fact hundreds of years later. He confirmed that the Lord said, "Your fathers, *including* Terah, the father of Abraham and the father of Nahor, dwelt on the other side of the River in old times; and *they served other gods"* (Joshua 24:2, emphasis supplied).

Abraham stood as a rock for the true God, encircled by the shifting sands of polytheism. His faith was as refreshing as a blooming oasis in the middle of the dry desert of heathenism. "Abraham was seemingly instrumental in breaking with the older polytheistic pattern of worshipping many gods to seek emphasis upon one God" (Kyle M. Yates, ed., *The Religious World,* p. 214).

Kenneth Oster, in his book *Islam Reconsidered,* emphasizes that monotheism "is a high mountain that must be scaled, not a valley into which man naturally slithers." Then he adds, "The natural man slides into polytheism as has been demonstrated so clearly throughout the history of the world" (pp. 29, 31). The Koran reveals that Abraham confronted his people's heathen worship head on: "Behold! he said to his father and to his people, what are these images to which ye are (so assiduously) devoted? They said, we found our fathers worshipping them" (Koran 21:52, 53).

Many persons blame unfavorable circumstances and evil environment for their unfaithfulness to God. Naturally such things make it difficult to follow Him; however, there is no power in the world that can stop a sincere person from coming wholeheartedly to God. "Idolatry invited him on every side, but in vain. Faithful among the faithless, uncorrupted by the prevailing apostasy, he steadfastly adhered to the worship of the one true God" (*Patriarchs and Prophets,* p. 125).

That is why it is not surprising to see how willing Abraham was to leave everything behind him and go wherever God wanted him to go. He was not even sure where he was to go, but he was sure of his God. Accompanied by his wife Sarah; his father Terah; Nahor, one of his two older brothers, and his wife Milcah; and Lot, his young nephew, the son of Haran, his deceased older brother, Abraham headed in faith to Haran. After living in the relative security of Haran for some years, Terah died of old age, and Nahor decided to discontinue the uncertain and risky journey toward the land of Canaan.

God again called Abraham to leave his home, and to go to "a land that I will show you" (Gen. 12:1). This time his family was diminished, for only Sarah and Lot accompanied him on this journey of no return. Those of us who have had the experience of being called to leave home and friends and go to a foreign field begin to understand how Abraham must have felt. At least we know where we are going and have a good idea as to what we will be doing when we get to our destination. But Abraham only knew his God, and he trusted in Him and His providence.

Moreover, Abraham is known as the father of faith because he acted on that faith in God. The apostle Paul combines these two interrelating elements: faith and obedience. Writes he, "By *faith* Abraham *obeyed* when he was called to go out to the place which he would afterward receive as an inheritance. And he went out *not knowing where he was going*" (Heb. 11:8 emphasis supplied).

From Haran, Abraham journeyed to Shechem in the land of Canaan, wandering in the desert as a nomad. He finally pitched his tents under the shade of the oaks of Morch for some time before he was to start his sojourn all over again. What a marked contrast he experienced between the leisure and security of the advanced urban centers of Ur and Haran, and the unsettled life of a nomad.

The site of the ancient city of Ur is the present-day town of Muqaiyar in Iraq, located about 150 miles southeast of old Babylon, and the same distance northwest of the Persian Gulf. The Jewish scholar Isidore Epstein described the location of Ur as "half-way between Baghdad and the head of the Persian Gulf, some ten miles west of the present course of the Euphrates" (*Judaism*, p. 11).

Excavations in early and mid parts of the last century revealed that both Ur and Haran enjoyed the luxuries of well constructed two-story houses equipped with central courtyards and indoor plumbing connected to a city sewage system. After more than 3,800 years, imagine that the houses then were even more fashionable and opulent than the houses on the same sites today.

Today Haran lies close to Balikh River, a tributary of the Euphrates River in northern Syria. At least in a minute way, I can imagine how Abraham must have felt leaving all his familiar associations in that city and venturing into the unknown vastness of the wilderness. As a youngster, I too had to abandon my relatives and familiar associations to emigrate to the United States. Abraham's solid faith inspired my fledgling faith in the same changeless God. It was painful to bid farewell to my loved ones. The future seemed uncertain as I left my small town located approximately 200 miles west of Haran on the east side of the Mediterranean Sea, and west of the Euphrates River.

Many incidents in Abraham's life show his trust in God and faithfulness to Him. His relationship with God resulted from an intimate and mutual friendship between them. One cannot always understand everything about one's true friend, but that does not undermine the friendship, because it is grounded in genuine love, trust, and esteem. They both knew each other and conversed together as close friends do.

We remember the familiar story of the three angels visiting with Abraham, and One of them was the divine Son of God. From the personal interaction in Genesis 18:16-33, it is clear that the Lord and Abraham were close friends indeed. After the two angels departed, the Lord had a special One-on-one conversation with him. He introduced His discussion of the fate of Sodom and Gomorrah by affirming that He was acquainted with Abraham as a friend, and therefore He could not hide from him His plans. And Abraham seemed free to share his ideas and even "bargain" with the Lord in his effort to mediate in behalf of the righteous.

When friends truly know each other well, they are free and confident to discuss things back and forth, and to trust each other with their secrets. It is awesome to realize that we, frail human beings, may have this type of friendship with our Creator! "Angels of heaven walked and talked with him as *friend with friend.* . . . Two of the heavenly messengers departed, leaving Abraham alone with Him whom he now knew to be the Son of God" (*Patriarchs and Prophets,* pp. 138, 139, emphasis supplied; see also 2 Chronicles 20:7; Isaiah 41:8; and James 2:23).

Yes, there are his literal genetic descendants, namely the Jews, the Arabs, and the early Christian Church, which emerged from literal Israel. Of course we know from history that Christianity rapidly spread to many non-Jewish nations in the Roman Empire. Consequently, Gentile Christians cannot claim to be literal descendants of Abraham as such, but they continue in the sacred history of the Hebrews and are indeed his spiritual descendants.

Abraham was called to bless *all* the families and *all* the nations of the earth (see Genesis 12:3; 18:18) regardless of national origin, race, or color. You see, God is not One who is partial, narrow-minded, or exclusive in implementing His divine plan for the human race. He did not single out Abraham merely for the sake of Abraham, but much more for the sake of saving all of His precious creatures made in His image.

In commenting on the dual roles which Abraham played in the historical as well as the spiritual realms, Dutch theologian Henry Renckens writes, "Abraham was more than a historical figure. He was a biblical figure—the representative figure of the people of God and of the believer of all times. In a word, he was the father of faith" (ibid., p. 70).

So if Abraham is the father of the faithful, then of whom is he the father? Who are his true descendants? John the Baptist, in preparing the way for the Messiah, challenged the Jewish leaders' claim of and false security in being Abraham's children without bearing fruit worthy of repentance. They had the presumptuous idea that they totally monopolized Abraham and could confine God's plan, regardless of their behavior. So John the Baptist laid bare their false

17

pretensions in warning them thus: "Do not think to say to your-selves, 'We have Abraham as *our* father.' For I say to you that God is able to raise up children to Abraham from these stones" (Matthew 3:9, emphasis supplied).

Later on, Jesus Himself confronted them by explaining what it means to be the true seed of Abraham. "They answered and said to Him, 'Abraham is our father.' Jesus said to them, 'If you were Abraham's children, you would do the works of Abraham' " (John 8:39). And Jesus continued with this strong reproof, fully aware that they were conspiring to murder Him, the true Seed of Abraham. "You are of your father the devil, and the desires of your father you want to do" (verse 44).

The Talmud, the authoritative body of Jewish traditions, records the presumption that the Jews were the only ones chosen for salvation to the exclusion of all others. There we find a revealing story of Abraham supposedly serving as a gatekeeper to the entrance of heaven. He stands there making sure that only the Israelites enter and vigilantly keeps out all the others.

A former Pharisee himself, the apostle Paul clarified that Abraham is the father of *all* those who walk in the steps of father Abraham and truly believe in his God and do His righteous works. He writes that Abraham "received the sign of circumcision, a seal of the righteous-ness of the faith which he had while still uncircumcised, that he might be the father of all those who believe, though they are uncir-cumcised . . . and the father of circumcision to those who not only are of the circumcision, but who also walk in the steps of the faith which our father Abraham had while still uncircumcised" (Romans 4:11, 12). Consequently, salvation through the righteousness of faith is certain to *all* the seed of Abraham, to "those who are of the faith of Abraham, who is the *father of us all*"(verse 16, emphasis supplied).

This reminds me of our faithful watchman Muhammed, who served us so well while we were working as missionaries in West Africa. He was a devout, diligent, and loyal Muslim from Burkina Faso (formerly Upper Volta). As I became better acquainted with him, I was surprised to learn that he had been a Christian before converting to Islam. When asked why he made this radical change in his life, he answered in a way I will never forget. "Christians all around me in my village would drink, smoke, and be involved in all sorts of immoral activities," he explained. "So I decided to become a Muslim, because Muslims pray to God continuously, and try to live a clean and moral life before Him." Then he concluded by saying that he wanted to be a godly man, a true son of Abraham, so that he would be ready for the judgment that was coming upon the world.

His explanation is etched in my mind, obviously not because Muslims and Christians are more or less righteous than each other, but because of his motivation for change. And this is what Jesus had in mind when He emphasized that to be a genuine descendant of Abraham and to be a true son of God is to do Abraham's righteous works (see John 8:39, 44). As I shared with Muhammed what the Bible says about being a son of Abraham, I also shared with him this relevant text from his holy book, the Koran: "Abraham was not a Jew, nor yet a Christian; but he was true in faith, and bowed his will to God's. . . . Without doubt, among men, the nearest of kin to Abraham, are those who follow him" (Koran 3:67, 68).

CHAPTER
2

The Seed of Abraham

At the height of the terrible civil war in Lebanon, atrocities were being committed by various warring factions, mostly against innocent civilians. There is a certain incongruity between such abhorrent acts of violence among the contemporary sons of Abraham and the seal of circumcision alluded to in Genesis 17. God gave Abraham this sign of circumcision to seal His relationship of love and trust between Himself and all of Abraham's descendants. So in obedience to God, Abraham and his son Ishmael were circumcised, along with all the men of their household (see Genesis 17:10-27; Romans 4:11, 12).

This sign of circumcision is ironic in today's setting, for in Lebanon it became a sign of distrust and even bloodshed. Battling Christian and Muslim militias, itching for revenge against each other, would set roadblocks and stop vehicles in order to ascertain who belonged to what faction. In Lebanon, the Muslims practice circumcision, however, the Christians generally do not. A reliable way to identify Christians from Muslims was to strip naked the male passengers; their life or death depended on what religious militia stopped them that day.

War is diabolic and insane, for it unleaches the very worst in mankind. Moreover, the bitter violence that went on unabated in Lebanon of brother against brother shows how very far from the ideal of father Abraham his descendants have reached.

This conflict is by no means limited to the children of Abraham in Lebanon, but it pervades the territories of the West Bank and the Gaza Strip where Israelis and Palestinians continue to battle and exact revenge against each other. The Palestinian young people call their uprising the *intifadah,* which refers to the call to rid themselves of the Israeli yoke of subjugation, a yoke which many of them have grimly en-dured from birth. Samir Kafity, Anglican bishop of Jerusalem and the Middle East, explained that this Arabic word *intifadah* is "the same word that Christ used when he instructed his disciples to shake off the dust from cities rejecting them" (Kim A. Lawton, "An Elusive Peace," *Christianity Today* [April 21, 1989], p. 34).

In this age of satellite telecommunications, millions of people watched in their own living rooms as armed Israeli soldiers battled with stone-throwing Palestinian youth. These young people were willing to risk their lives and to die by the hundreds for what they believed to be their just cause of liberty and self determination.

People worldwide are asking whether David and Goliath have reversed their roles in this present-day conflict between the Israelis and the Palestinians, whether the oppressed people have indeed now taken their turn of becoming the oppressors. Of all peoples on the face of earth, it seems that the Jews should be most able to sympathize with others who are deprived, displaced, and dispersed.

A revealing article by Carl Bernstein explains how the plight of Palestinians is troubling the conscience of many American Jews, who are now questioning Israel's repressive policies towards them. "The American Jewish community has become a house divided—and sometimes loudly so—over Israel's treatment of Palestinians in the occupied areas and its reluctance to pursue a comprehensive settlement that finally might bring peace to the region" ("The Agony Over Israel," *Time*, [May 7, 1990], p. 28).

Bernstein goes on to quote John Ruskay of the Jewish Theological Seminary as lamenting: "The sadness is that after 40 years and a Holocaust we end up occupying thousands of Palestinians against their will" (ibid.). Finally he quotes Albert Vorspan, the senior vice president of the Union of American Hebrew Congregations, as saying that "if Jews in Israel are divided almost down the middle over the Palestinian question, American Jews are going to be divided as well" (ibid., pp. 29, 30).

"I was walking down a street and I saw this little boy—I think he was a boy—he wasn't much more than one year old," a dismayed Israeli brigadier general begins, telling an experience he had during the *intifada*. "He had just learned to walk. He had a stone in his hand. He could barely hold on to it, but he was walking around with a stone to throw at someone. I looked at him and he looked at me, and I smiled and he dropped the stone. I think it was probably too heavy for him."

Refecting on this incident with this stone-carrying Palestinian child, the general said, "For that little kid, anger is a part of his life, a part of growing up—as much as talking or eating. He still didn't know exactly against whom he was angry; he was too young for that. He will know after a while. But for now he kew he was supposed to be angry. He knew he was supposed to throw a stone at someone" (Friedman, p. 374).

It is hard to imagine that after thousands of years, such jealousies and conflicts are still in existance, and unfortunately they are getting worse. These animosities may be traced all the way back to the time when Abraham and Sarah impatiently tried to fulfill God's promise of a son by their own human devising. It certainly gives us courage to know that even Abraham, the father of faith and the friend of God, had to grow in his faith. Along the path of his growth in faith, he made some mistakes for which his posterity still suffers the consequences. Yet God, in His wisdom and mercy, tried to work things out for the good by making the most out of a less than ideal situation.

On more than one occasion, God promised Abraham that He would give him many descendants through his own son of promise. But through which son? Why not his beloved firstborn son Ishmael ("God hears")? Apparently God was not satisfied with Abraham's human plan in fulfilling His eternal covenant. And that was the reason why afterward God twice reaffirmed (see Genesis 17:19 and 18:10) His promise of giving Abraham and Sarah their very own son, regardless of their advanced age of one hundred years and ninety years, respectively. But they were not to worry about their age, because God assured them that there was nothing too hard for Him to accomplish (see Genesis 18:14).

Sometimes Hagar is viewed in a negative light in this discussion of the son of promise. However, it was not her idea, but Sarah's, to become Abraham's secondary wife. Ten years had already passed by since God had promised them a son, and they were becoming impatient, waiting for Him to act. We can imagine the countless times they had discussed this matter back and forth. Finally, Sarah, feeling the bulk of the responsibility for not bearing her husband a son (see Genesis 16:1, 2), not only introduced Abraham to this scheme, but she herself also "took Hagar her maid, the Egyptian, and gave her to her husband Abram to be his wife" (verse 3).

If there was any blame (and there was), it was to fall squarely on Sarah and Abraham. For instead of patiently heeding the counsel of God, they continued to follow the customs and legal codes of Hammurabi from the land they had left behind. Such codes stated that a childless wife could give one of her maids to her husband as a secondary wife, whereby she could obtain an heir to carry the family's heritage and inheritance (see *SDA Bible Commentary*, vol. 1, p. 317).

Lest we be tempted to have a blame-it-on-Eve attitude by being too hard on Sarah, let us recall that earlier Abraham himself had tried to circumvent God's plan by contemplating to make his faithful servant Eliezer of Damascus his heir (see Genesis 15:4, 5). He tried to find fulfillment to God's promise in his Syrian servant, just as Sarah attempted to find it in Hagar. It was an acceptable custom at the time to adopt one's trusted servant to be the legal son and heir. This provided a way out, according to ancient records from Nuzi, for a childless family (ibid., p. 312).

It's remarkable how unfaltering God was in His patience with His friends Abraham and Sarah. With great love and forbearance, which could only spring forth from His generous heart, He was teaching them the essential lessons of complete submission to Him and unwavering trust in His providence. In dealing with Abraham and Sarah, God had a divine design for bringing salvation to the whole world, and He wanted to make sure, even from the inception of this eternal plan, that every facet of it was going to be right. Not only was God's gift of the miracle child Isaac to be founded on implicit faith and trust in Him, but also the entire covenant relationship with his descendants was to be anchored in the same.

Some might imagine that because God chose Isaac, the son of Abraham and Sarah, to be the son of promise, He somehow rejected Ishmael and his descendants. However, it is evident from the Scriptures that such a supposition is not solidly founded. After all, how about Esau? He was the son of Isaac and the grandson of Abraham and Sarah. Consider the sons of Jacob. Wasn't Joseph the great-grandson of Abraham and Sarah? And didn't he possess an impeccable character? Of course he did. But the Lord in His wisdom and sovereignty chose his half-brother Judah, the son of his Aunt Leah, as the ancestor of the Messiah. God's concern in His selection is not limited to one person. Rather, His supreme concern is for the blessing and salvation of all humanity. But through one person, one people, He needed to convey His message of redemption to the whole world.

Ellen White comments that as a consequence of Ishmael's departure, Abraham "was thrown into great distress. How could he banish . . . his son, still dearly beloved?" The patriarch obeyed the Lord in letting Ishmael leave, but "it was not without keen suffering. The father's heart was heavy with unspoken grief as he sent away Hagar and his son" (*Patriarchs and Prophets*, pp. 146, 147).

Though Ishmael was conceived as a result of Abraham's and Sarah's distrust of God's plan, nevertheless God promised to greatly bless him and his descendants. God said of Ishmael: "Behold, I have blessed him, and will make him fruitful, and will multiply him exceedingly. He shall beget twelve princes, and I will make him a great nation" (Genesis 17:20). He repeated the same promise to Abraham and Hagar in Genesis 16:10-12; and 21:13, 18. God watched over him as he prospered in the wilderness of Paran, located between the Gulfs of Aqaba and Suez in the south of Palestine. In due time, Ishmael's mother helped him find a wife from her native land of Egypt (see chapter 21:20, 21).

God was faithful in fulfilling His promise to Ishmael by blessing him with twelve sons of Semitic and Egyptian ancestry. It is hard to miss the similarity of God's blessing to Jacob and his uncle Ishmael with the same number of descendants. Each one was given twelve sons. The names of Ishmael's sons and tribes are mentioned in Genesis 25:12-16. These tribes roamed the whole region of Arabia, eastern Syria, and Jordan, and established powerful and prosperous kingdoms. We know that the Ishmaelites were industrious traders, driving their caravans all the way back to Egypt, Hagar's homeland.

Years later, these relatives of Jacob, accompanied by the Midianites, passed by his sons, who were tending their flocks in Dothan. There in Dothan, situated on the caravan route to Egypt, Joseph was sold for twenty shekels of silver as a slave to these traders. In this account recorded in Genesis 37:27, 28, a group of Midianite traders were in business with the Ishmaelites. These two groups were cousins, for Ishmael and Midian were sons of Abraham. After the death of Sarah, Abraham married Keturah and was blessed with

25

six sons, of whom Midian was the fourth. The descendants of these sons still live in Syria, Egypt, Lebanon, Jordan, and parts of North Africa.

When Moses fled from Egypt and braved the Sinai desert, he finally settled in "the land of Midian" (see Exodus 2:15-21) and married Zipporah, one of the seven daughters of Reuel (also known as Jethro in Exodus 3:1), the priest of Midian. Philip Hitti, a specialist in the history of the Middle East, describes Zipporah as an Arab woman: "In Midian, the southern part of Sinai and the land east of it, the divine covenant was made. Moses, the leader of the tribes, there married an Arabian woman, the daughter of a Midianite priest" (*The Arabs: A Short Story*, p. 24).

The name Reuel means "friend of God" in Hebrew (the same title given to Abraham), which implies that he was a believer in the God of his ancestor Abraham, and a devout and wise priest of the true God (Exodus 18:12). For many years this godly prince and priest provided wise counsel to his son-in-law Moses.

Esau, at the age of forty, took two Hittite wives—Judith and Bashemath (Genesis 26:34, 35). Later on, Esau, knowing that his marriage to these Canaanite women displeased his parents, took a daughter of Ishmael, to be another wife (see 28:8, 9; 36:3). The terms *Canaanite* and *Hittite* are sometimes used interchangeably. The Greeks called them "Phoenicians" literally meaning "red purple," linking such appropriate terminology with "Edom," Esau's other name. For the name Edom literally meaning "red" in Hebrew, hearkening back to Esau selling his birthright to his brother Jacob for a stew of red lentils (see 25:29-34).

These descendants of Esau and his three wives were called the Edomites, and settled in southern Palestine and in the regions of west Arabah. Kenneth Oster writes that Esau, Isaac's firstborn, "closed the gap between the Arabs and Jews (though not called by those terms at that time) somewhat by marrying Bashemath, the daughter of Ishmael, sister of the twelve sons of Ishmael. . . . From this union sprang Reuel" (Oster, p. 14), who was the same person as Jethro, the father-in-law and counselor of Moses.

The above are just a few examples of the numerous interrelations and interactions between the many descendants and relatives of patriarch Abraham. That is why almost all the peoples of the Middle East take great pride in claiming him as their father. After so many years of turmoil, it is obvious that no real peace will ever come to that region unless its peoples show consideration and understanding toward each other in the spirit of Abraham.

It is in that spirit of reconciliation that one son of Abraham, the late president Anwar el-Sadat of Egypt, greatly desired to fulfill a dream of erecting a monument of peace at Mount Sinai for Jews, Christians, and Muslims for that region, and for the world. Sadat's commitment to peace led to his assassination in October of 1981, but not before his signing of a peace treaty (the Camp David accords) with the Israelis in September of 1978. At the signing ceremonies of the peace accords, it was impressive to see the three leaders: Menachem Begin (Jew), Anwar el-Sadat (Muslim), Jimmy Carter (Christian) representing the children of Abraham in clasped hands of reconciliation.

President Carter deserves the gratitude of the world for his crusade for peace in the Middle East. He knew Sadat well and knew that the president of Egypt was thoroughly acquainted with the ancient historical relationship linking his people and the children of Israel. Carter and Sadat often discussed this vital subject.

Carter's intensive search for peace in that region and his extensive visits there resulted in an informative book entitled *The Blood of Abraham*. In it he relates that Sadat "mentioned frequently, and almost casually, the brotherhood of Arab and Jew and how they are both the sons of Abraham" (Carter, p. 5). This caused President Carter to reexamine simultaneously the biblical story of Abraham and his descendants from Jewish, Christian, and Muslim perspectives (ibid.).

Jehan Sadat (born in Egypt of an Egyptian Muslim father and of an English Christian mother), the widow of the late President

Sadat, recently wrote her memoirs in which she presented her views from an informed Muslim perspective. She writes that "Isaac's descendants in Palestine would develop the faith of Israel and that of Christ, while Isma'il's [Ishmael's] descendants in Arabia would perfect the faith of Islam. Because Isaac and Isma'il were both sons of Ibrahim [Abraham], we say that Sarah is Mother of the Jews and the Christians while Hagar is Mother of the Muslims, and that all of us Muslims, Christians and Jews, are cousins" (*A Woman of Egypt*, p. 277).

While circling over the 7,500-foot peak of Mount Sinai, President Carter remembered the several animated discussions President Sadat had with him about a shrine of peace for the three great monotheistic religions (see Carter, pp. 155, 156). Unfortunately, Sadat's untimely death did not permit him to fulfill this dream, but I believe the idea serves to remind us again that real peace can come only from the Source of peace. The God of Abraham was the same God who gave Moses the moral and universal law of the Ten Commandments, which is the only basis for human harmony.

3

The Son of Promise
Part One

A car abruptly screeched to a halt at a street curb in war-torn west Beirut one Sunday afternoon, and there emerged a haggard-looking American surrounded by heavily armed men. He was promptly jostled into a bulletproof Syrian car waiting across the street, and whisked off to Damascus. That was Dr. Robert Polhill, a professor at Beirut University College, who was abducted on campus and held hostage for more than three agonizing years by a group calling itself the Islamic Holy War for the Liberation of Palestine.

Interestingly enough, his wife, Ferial Polhill, is a Palestinian by birth. But despite her national origin, her incessant efforts to effect the release of her innocent husband, and the Polhills' unreserved acceptance of and commitment to serve the local people, the abductors obstinately kept the agriculture professor in prolonged captivity (see Richard Lacayo, "Games Captors Play," *Time* [April 30, 1990], pp. 32, 33). Another American hostage, Dr. Frank Reed, was released a week after Polhill and handed over to the Syrian authorities in Damascus. He was wholeheartedly devoted to the education of the Lebanese youth. In fact, he is a convert to Islam, and his wife Fahima is Syrian-born.

Unfortunately, several American hostages had remained in captivity for more than six years. Terry Anderson was one of those brave hostages. No one who observed his devoted sister, Mrs. Peggy Say, could help but be greatly inspired by her positive attitude. For many years she unrelentingly championed her brother's cause against many formidable odds. She visited many heads of state in the Middle East and doggedly pursued any channel in the hope of exerting some influence on the fate of Terry and the other hostages.

In an inspiring interview, she asserted that no matter what the circumstances might be, she would never give up. Despite all that happened to her brother, she was not bitter, she added. She was hopeful that this trying ordeal would actually do some good, by compelling the conflicting parties to bring peace to that troubled part of the world.

Peggy Say's unshakable fortitude and commitment to the liberation of her brother and all oppressed people remind us of another liberator. Abraham and his servants courageously pursued a federation of five kings who had raided Sodom and took prisoners, including Abraham's nephew Lot and many others. Abraham relentlessly pursued them all the way north to Damascus. When he wrested the hostages away from their captors and returned them safely with the stolen goods to Sodom, the king of Sodom wanted to give him a reward. He offered to reimburse Abraham with all the recovered goods, but he would not accept any form of payment for this noble deed which God had empowered him to accomplish (see Genesis 14:11-24).

Why isn't the spirit of Abraham evident among his children today? I believe the basic reason is that temporal freedom must proceed from spiritual freedom of the human soul. And this kind of freedom comes only from its true Source—the true Son and Seed of Abraham.

It was this Source who said, "If the Son makes you free, you shall be free indeed" (John 8:36). This Son of Abraham and Son of God also said this of Himself, "The Spirit of the Lord God is upon Me, because the Lord has anointed Me to preach good tidings to the poor; He has sent Me to heal the brokenhearted, to proclaim liberty to the captives, and the opening of the prison to those who are bound" (Isaiah 61:1). He is the One who brings liberty from the shackles of sin that hold people hostage to hatred and revenge. He is the One who is known throughout the Bible to bring people out of bondage.

He is the One who called Moses to go from the desert of Sinai to the land of Egypt to liberate the children of Israel from their abject slavery. Moses himself and the children of Israel serve as types of Jesus. Just as God called His people out of Egypt, so also He later called His Son Jesus out of the same country.

Jacob and his sons sojourned in Egypt, fleeing the ravages of famine in Canaan. The Kyksos rulers of Egypt were of Semitic origins, just as the Israelites; and this probably explains the amicable relations between them (see William Shea, "Leaving Egypt," *Adventist Review* [May 17, 1990], p. 10).

Notice the dual application in this connection between Israel and Jesus evident in Exodus 4:22, 23. God instructs Moses to say thus to Pharaoh: "Israel is My son, My firstborn. So I say to you, let My son go that he may serve Me." Under divine inspiration, Matthew applies the words of Hosea 11:1 to God's only Son, Jesus. He writes that Jesus and His parents remained in Egypt until the death of Herod, "that it might be fulfilled which was spoken by the Lord through the prophet, saying, 'Out of Egypt I called My Son' " (Matthew 2:15).

Moreover, Moses himself, who demanded that Pharaoh (now a native Egyptian ruler) release the children of Israel from the bondage of slavery, was a forerunner or a type of Jesus, whom he depicted as a "Prophet like me," who would come to deliver His people from the bondage of sin. He gives such a prophetic promise to the people in his farewell address in Deuteronomy 18:15. "The Lord your God will raise up for you a Prophet like me from your midst, from your brethren. Him you shall hear." Then in verse 18, God Himself in similar words affirms Moses' prediction in promising: " 'I will raise up for them a Prophet like you from among their brethren, and will put My words in His mouth, and He shall speak to them all that I command Him.' "

This "Prophet," who was to be like Moses, was the One the Jews were awaiting (see John 6:14). He was the promised Messiah to bring salvation from sin. He was the Seed of the woman (see Genesis 3:15), whose heel was to be bruised by the serpent, but He was to finally crush its head. Similar imagery is used in Revelation 12:1-6, where the dragon (the old serpent, the Devil) was posed to destroy the male Child (Jesus) born of a woman (see Matthew 2:16). The apostle Peter makes the connection between this promised "Prophet" and the Seed of Abraham. This Seed in whom God was to bless the entire world, starting first with the literal children of Israel, was none other than His Son Jesus (see Acts 3:22-26).

The same singular form of the word *seed* is employed in Genesis 3:15 to indicate that the crux of the Great Controversy is between Christ and Satan. If that war between good and evil was ever going to be won, it was going to be won by Christ Himself, the Seed of the woman, on behalf of the human race. Christ did defeat Satan at the cross (see Hebrews 2:14-16), and He will finally destroy him at the end of the millennium (see Revelation 20:10).

The apostle Paul also makes a similar application of the singular term *seed* to refer to Christ as the Seed of Abraham. Referring back to the promise God made to Abraham in Genesis 22:18, he makes this Messianic application: "To Abraham and his Seed were the promises made," he writes. "He does not say, 'And to seeds,' as of many, but as of one, 'And to your Seed,' who is Christ" (Galatians

3:16). Though God made many promises to Abraham relating to his literal descendants and to the literal land he was to inherit, these were secondary to the primary purpose of the coming of the Messiah and His universal salvation of humanity. Through this salvation of Christ, the inheritance was not confined merely to literal Canaan, but extended too the entire earth.

God intended the children of Israel to be His instrument for the salvation of the world. They were to look beyond themselves as the chosen people of God to the salvation of all the children of God. They were to discern the Messiah, God's true Son of Promise, through the representative type of Isaac, Abraham's son of promise. Unfortunately, they were so obsessed with the immediate that they overlooked the eternal; they became so preoccupied with types and figures that they did not see the realities they represented. However, father Abraham himself, many years before their time, rejoiced in seeing what is real and eternal.

When the Jewish leaders cynically questioned Jesus as to whom He considered Himself to be, and if He were greater than their father Abraham, He answered them: "Your father Abraham rejoiced to see My day, and he saw it and was glad" (John 8:56). Moreover, God's promise of an earthly homeland did not blind Abraham's eyes to the ultimate fulfillment of receiving "a heavenly country" (Hebrews 11:16). With all the assurances of an earthly country, Abraham considered himself a stranger and a pilgrim on this earth (see verse 13), and did not forget that he was waiting for a heavenly city whose builder is God (verse 10).

Hans LaRondelle, in affirming how the promises made to Abraham find their ultimate fulfillment in the Messiah, writes: "Christ is the goal of the mission of Abraham and Israel. Christ came to redeem the world and the human race as a whole. Salvation is from the Jews but not for the Jews only" (*The Israel of God in Prophecy*, p. 18).

Isaac, the only miracle son of Abraham, is a type of Jesus, the only Son of God, just as Abraham serves as a type of God. Also the relationship that existed between this earthly father and son illustrates the intimate and eternal relationship which exists between God the Father and His Son Jesus. No other human relationship in the entire Bible represents so well the gospel.

Was God biased in choosing Isaac to prefigure the Saviour of the world? No, He was not at all biased, but God was determined to accomplish His divine plan through His own initiative based totally on a faith relationship with Abraham. He chose Isaac because he was the fulfillment of His original and often repeated promise, and because Isaac was a living demonstration of faith and of God's initiative. Abraham and Sarah tried to circumvent their essential trust in God and His initiative through their own works.

Some may think that God chose Isaac and not Ishmael simply because the latter's mother was a bondwoman. However, what about the choice of Jacob over Esau? Their origins were identical. In His wisdom and sovereignty, the all-knowing God has the prerogative of assigning different tasks to different individuals in order to accomplish His mission in the world.

By the time Isaac grew up to be a strong and godly young man of twenty, his father was 120 years old. And after the banishment of Ishmael seventeen years earlier, Isaac had proven to be his old parents' great solace and joy. Having tested their faith several times, God finally came through with His long-awaited promise of a son. At this very time they were probably anticipating the marriage of Isaac, praying that God would help them find just the right young woman for a wife for their son.

4

The Son of Promise
Part Two

The phone rang. A young mother was hysterically sobbing, imploring me to tell her what to do. "I just ran over my little boy with the car. I was hurriedly backing out of the garage, and I just had no idea that Timmy was playing behind the car!" Crying her heart out, she kept on, "He is our only child. Oh! What was the matter with me? How come I was not more careful?" Then, "Just what shall I tell my husband when he gets home?"

How can a parent possibly relate to causing the death of her own flesh and blood at her own hands, even though it all happened accidentally?

Such a tragic experience can help us understand how Abraham must have felt when he was asked to sacrifice his beloved son. Little did Abraham know the unexpected shock awaiting him. At this tranquil time, after seventeen long years of silence since Abraham received his last known message from God, he was to be subjected to the severest of human tests, "the closest which man was ever called to endure" (*Patriarchs and Prophets,* p. 147). In testing his faith, "God had reserved His last, most trying test for Abraham until the burden of years was heavy upon him, and he longed for rest from anxiety and toil" (ibid.).

Suddenly, God's commanding voice woke the old patriarch with this terrifying injunction: "Take now your son, your *only son* Isaac, whom you love, and go to the land of Moriah, and offer him there as a burnt offering on one of the mountains of which I shall tell you" (Genesis 22:2, emphasis supplied).

Was this a bad dream, a nightmare? Was this a cruel trick of the devil to unsettle his trust in God? Was this merely a passing hallucination brought about by the anxious heart of an old man? Why would this loving God, his best Friend in this world, seem to reverse Himself now in giving him this overwhelmingly severe command? The heathen gods of the Canaanites demanded such sacrifices, but why his God would make such an unreasonable demand defied human logic.

Ellen White states that at that trying time of Abraham's inner struggle, "Satan was at hand to suggest that he must be deceived, for the divine law commands, 'Thou shalt not kill,' and God would not require what He had once forbidden" (*Patriarchs and Prophets,* p. 148). But these difficult instances of questioning and uncertainty, when our souls are violently wrenched, are the very times when a genuine friendship between us and God really counts.

And that is exactly the kind of trusting relationship Abraham enjoyed with God. Obviously, God called him His friend for a good reason. Muslims join Jews and Christians in recognizing this honorable title which God bestowed on Abraham of being His special friend (see John T. Seamands, *Tell It Well,* p. 202). You see, Abraham had known God for many years, and He had repeatedly proven Himself to be totally trustworthy. This enduring friendship was in no way built on one isolated incident, but on the solid bonds forged during a lifelong commitment.

Abraham's test of faith was by no means an ordinary one. He was called upon in his old age to endure the most severe test of any human being. Isaac was a special son whom he greatly loved (see Genesis 22:2). He was the tangible and living evidence of God's faithfulness to him and to all of humanity. Every time he looked into his son's face he was reminded of this fact.

He longed at that time to unburden the anguish of his soul to Sarah, but he would not. He would bear this crushing burden alone, for Isaac was also his mother's "joy and pride; her life was bound up in him, and the mother's love might refuse the sacrifice" (*Patriarchs and Prophets*, p. 151).

Raïssa Maritain, in her thought-provoking article about Abraham's extraordinary ordeal, writes: "Without sparing, without preparation, the deadly command struck Abraham in the fullness of his joy. Isaac, the flowering of his trust, must be sacrificed: such was the incommunicable command, such the unique dialogue, such the lonely encounter with God. There was no escaping from mystery nor any help to hope for. For what God was demanding was something quite other than His usual demands: He demanded the impossible, and yet the impossible might not be refused Him" (Raïssa Maritain, "Abraham and the Ascent of Conscience," in *The Bridge*, ed. John M. Oesterreicher [New York: Pantheon, n.d.], vol. 1, p. 37).

Early the next morning, as Abraham and his son started their journey to the land of Moriah, Isaac assumed that it was simply another trip on which he accompanied his father. But this time his father seemed to be withdrawn and in deep thought. What appropriate words could come from a father's heart at such a time? "The patriarch, pondering his heavy secret, had no heart for words. His thoughts were of the proud, fond mother, and the day when he should return to her alone. Well he knew that the knife would pierce her heart when it took the life of her son" (*Patriarchs and Prophets*, p. 151). What words of encouragement would we have given Abraham during that severe crisis? The ordeal sapped the old man's emotions to the very core and fiercely pierced his heart.

Considering again God's command to Abraham recorded in Genesis 22:2, we can see some significant and specific parallels between Abraham and God, and between Isaac and Jesus, the Son of God. First of all, God refers to Isaac as Abraham's "only son." And the term *yachid* in Hebrew is used "in the absolute sense of aloneness, singly, individually" (F. C. Gilbert, *Practical Lessons,* p. 139). A similar word, *wahid,* is used in Arabic in reference to Isaac, and carries the same meaning as the Hebrew.

The NIV accurately translates this term in the familiar text of John 3:16. "For God so loved the world that he gave his *one and only Son,* that whoever believes in him shall not perish but have eternal life" (see also the references of John 1:18; 3:18; 1 John 4:9). Paul uses the Greek *monogenes* in Hebrew 11:17 as equivalent to the Hebrew *yachid* in Genesis 22:2 in describing Isaac, thereby linking Old and New Testament usage.

One may ask why Isaac was called the only son of Abraham. Wasn't Ishmael Abraham's firstborn? And didn't Abraham beget six other sons from his second wife Keturah? Yes, of course. Isaac was by no means the only begotten or the first begotten, but he was the only son of promise uniquely eligible to be the covenant heir and inherit Abraham's birthright. God's plan from the beginning was that the rightful heir would come from *both* Abraham and Sarah. God remained faithful to this plan, despite their attempt to fulfill His divine plan in their own human way.

The inaccurate translation of the Greek word *monogenes* to mean "begotten" rather than "only," or "one of a kind," originated with the early religious leaders of the Catholic Church such as Origen and Arius (see *Problems in Bible Translations,* pp. 197-202). This inaccuracy has contributed to considerable theological misconception among many people, Christian and otherwise, particularly the Muslims. They shun this idea of God's begetting a son, especially in the light of the Catholic Church's elevation of Mary to deity as the

Mother of God. And in defense of absolute monotheism the Koran declares: "Say: He is God, the One and Only; God, the Eternal, Absolute; He begetteth not, nor is He begotten; and there is none like unto Him" (Koran 112:2-4).

Another parallel is that both Isaac and the incarnate Christ were *miraculously conceived.* It was physically impossible for Sarah to have a child because of her advanced age of ninety years. But the Lord kept His promise, and at the appointed time, He visited Sarah and transformed her barren womb into a fruitful one, for nothing is "too hard for the Lord" (see Genesis 18:14; 21:1, 2). Jesus was a miracle Child in His incarnation. Mary was yet a young virgin when the angel Gabriel came to break the startling news to her. That is why she asked him how this could possibly be since she was still a virgin. That is when Gabriel announced to her that "the Holy Spirit will come upon you, and that Holy One who is to be born will be called the Son of God" (Luke 1:35).

The Koran, the Muslims' holy book, seems to concur with the Luke account of the miraculous conception of Christ (who is called Isa). "She [Mary] said: 'How shall I have a son, seeing that no man has touched me, and I am not unchaste?' He [Gabriel] said: 'So (it will be): Thy Lord saith, "That is easy for Me, and (We wish) to appoint him (Jesus) as a Sign unto men, and a Mercy from us" ' " (Koran 19:20, 21). The Koran applies some special titles to Jesus that it does not apply to any other prophet. Notice the title of a "*Sign* unto men," which is in accordance with the Messianic prophecy recorded in Isaiah 7:14. "The Lord Himself will give you a *sign:* Behold, the virgin shall conceive and bear a Son, and shall call His name Immanuel."

Another parallel is found in Abraham's willingness to deliver up his son Isaac as a sacrifice (see Genesis 22:9, 10) and in God the Father, "who did not spare His own Son, but *delivered Him up* for us all" (Romans, 8:32, emphasis supplied).

The Muslims commemorate this event by celebrating the Feast of Sacrifice, to honor Abraham's complete submission to God in being willing to sacrifice his son. Thus the Arabic term *Islam* literally means "submission (to God)," implying that all true followers of God emulate the example of Abraham. And that is precisely the experience all the children of Abraham must possess—to trust God and surrender their lives completely to Him.

Another parallel is in connection with Mount Moriah, where Abraham was to offer his son Isaac. One possible translation of the word *Moriah* is "the place where God will appear and provide." Moreover, this was the location west of the Kidron Valley where Solomon built the temple (see 2 Chronicles 3:1). Animal sacrifices were offered in that temple, pointing forward to the great sacrifice of Christ on nearby Mount Golgotha (see John 19:17).

The Muslim Dome of the Rock presently sits on Mount Moriah and marks the spot where Solomon's temple used to be. This is one of the most sacred sites to many millions of Muslims around the world, because they believe that this was the location of the sacred "rock" (hence Dome of the Rock). In contrast to the Judeo-Christian story of the sacrifice of Isaac, Muslims believe that Abraham was willing to sacrifice his son Ishmael at this site. In addition, Mohammed reputedly ascended on his horse to heaven here (see David and John Noss, *A History of the World's Religions,* p. 544).

The rich heritage surrounding this mount has given Jews and Muslims more opportunity for conflict, as demonstrated by the death of twenty-one Palestinians on October 15, 1990. "Violence courts violence in a perpetual magic circle," says Meron Benvenisti, former deputy mayor of Jerusalem. "And at its heart, a time bomb with a destructive force of apocalyptic dimensions is ticking, in the form of the Temple Mount" (Charles Lane, "A Time Bomb at the City's Heart," *Newsweek* [October 22, 1990], p. 38).

A parallel exists in relation to the father-son dialogue that must have pierced Abraham's heart. Isaac eventually asked his father the decisive question he had held back to the very end. "My father! . . . Look, the fire and the wood, but where is the lamb for a burnt offering?" With an anguished, yet trusting heart, Abraham managed to answer, "My son, God will provide for Himself the lamb for a burnt offering" (Genesis 22:7, 8). How prophetic were the words of Abraham! Indeed that was what transpired; for God did provide a substitutionary sacrificial lamb then, and would provide the substitutionary sacrificial lamb of His Son Jesus at Calvary.

Abraham apparently began to see by faith a glimmer of hope beyond the perplexing situation. Even as "he bound Isaac his son and laid him on the altar, upon the wood" (Genesis 22:9), he hoped that his God of the impossible would provide a way out. And even if Isaac were to die, God would be more than able to bring him back to life. Christ Himself was bound with cords, and shortly after, He was bound again with nails on a wooden cross (see John 18:12; 20:25).

Abraham's faith in God was tested to the limit. Tightly pressed on every side by this torturing ordeal, and with no satisfying answers to the puzzlements of his pain-riddled heart, he knew that God had things under control. Many things he did not know, but he knew that his best Friend God was thoroughly trustworthy, and He would bring about the right and best outcome under these trying circumstances.

The apostle Paul explains that when Abraham offered up Isaac, he believed that God "was able to raise him up, even from the dead, from which he also received him in a figurative sense" (Hebrews 11:19). But Abraham's heart had to be knit with God's heart to accomplish this act of heroic faith. "Only thus could the aged patriarch reconcile God's promise that Isaac was to be his heir, with God's mandate to take Isaac's life. To have faith in the integrity of a person who makes a promise and a demand that seem to be so mutually exclusive is *the ultimate in the perfection of faith*" (*SDA Bible Commentary*, vol. 7, p. 475, emphasis supplied).

We may be bold enough to affirm that such an act is humanly possible, not because of any merit in Abraham or us, but simply because we have faith in our God, and "being fully convinced that what He had promised He was also able to perform" (Romans

4:21). However, this results *only* through the intimate union of the human and divine. For "as the will of man co-operates with the will of God, it becomes *omnipotent. Whatever* is to be done at *His command* may be accomplished in *His strength. All* His biddings are enablings" (*Christ's Object Lessons,* p. 333, emphasis supplied).

And that's what God wanted Abraham to understand. God wanted to share His own feelings about His turn of giving up His own beloved Son as the ultimate Sacrifice for the world. In that sense, God chose Abraham for that honorable position of becoming His type of a father, just as He chose Isaac to be the type of His Son Jesus. C. K. Barrett explains that God's willingness to raise Isaac from the dead was a figure of Christ's resurrection. He writes: "That which the Old Testament foreshadowed has become manifest in the death and resurrection of Jesus, in which God raised up his own Son not from a dead womb but from the grave" (*Harper's N.T. Commentaries: The Epistle to the Romans,* p. 99).

Abraham could tell his son, "God will provide for Himself the lamb," and God did: but here God the Father could not find an adequate substitute for His beloved and only son. Why? Because Christ Himself was that sacrificial and substitutionary "Lamb slain from the foundation of the world" (Revelation 13:8). Even to the very end, Isaac did not know what was awaiting him, for his loving father longed to spare him any undue pain. However, Christ knew from eternity that He was to offer Himself as the ultimate Sacrifice for the fallen human race.

Even long before the fall of man, Christ contemplated His voluntary sacrifice in giving Himself to redeem lost humanity. We are told that "the plan for our redemption was not an afterthought, a plan formulated after the fall of Adam." In the councils of God in heaven, Christ stepped forward to volunteer Himself as the Sacrifice to meet the emergence of sin, and He covenanted with His Father to pay that ultimate price in behalf of the human race (see *The Desire of Ages,* p. 22).

That type of cooperation, trust, and unity was typical of Abraham and his son. And this brings us to the final parallel. Isaac was a strong twenty-year-old young man, full of the vigor of youth. He could have easily resisted his aged father, especially weakened by the ordeal of the last three days. But Isaac apparently volunteered to cooperate with his father in being offered as a sacrifice to God. Although he was stunned at what his father planned to do in obeying God's command, he offered no protest nor waged any kind of struggle.

Naturally, he could easily have escaped his fate, considering his father's physical weakness and the seemingly illogical and unreasonable command. After all, it was his own life on the line. Amazingly, Isaac not only submitted to God's will and to his father's faith in Him, but he even strengthened the old man's trembling hands. We are often amazed at Abraham's tenacious faith, but Isaac's faith was also great. As a type of Christ, he exhibited faith and love that impelled him to be submissive and obedient, even unto death.

Robert Wieland puts it aptly when he writes: "The father's faith and devotion were perfectly reflected or equalled by the son's. The father so loved that he gave his son, and the son so loved that he gave himself! The world has never seen such a demonstration of love, such whole-hearted devotion to God on the part of both a human father and son" (*In Search of the Treasure of Faith,* p. 91).

God the Father so loved that He gave His only Son (see John 3:16), and God the Son so loved that He submitted Himself voluntarily to give Himself for fallen humanity. Jesus was "oppressed and He was afflicted, yet He opened not His mouth; He was led as a lamb to the slaughter, and as a sheep before its shearers is silent, so He opened not His mouth" (Isaiah 53:7).

Moreover, just as Isaac was to be sacrificed at the hands of his father, so also was Christ our Substitute to suffer death under the full weight of God's divine justice. No human hand could have been laid on Christ, had it not been for Him and His Father mutually agreeing beforehand that Christ would bear the crushing burden of all humanity's sins. It was the sin of the whole world, your sin and mine, that killed Jesus. "But it was not the spear thrust, it was not the pain of the cross, that caused the death of Jesus. . . . He died of a broken heart. His heart was broken by mental anguish. *He was slain by the sin of the world*" (*The Desire of Ages,* p. 772, emphasis supplied). The prophet Isaiah declares this of Christ: "He was wounded for our transgressions, He was bruised for our iniquities. . . . And the Lord has laid on Him the iniquity of *us all*" (Isaiah 53:3, 6, emphasis supplied).

Just as the Father and Son clasped hands together in a solemn pledge that Christ would die to save humanity, so also Isaac's strong hands clasped his father's trembling hands to courageously fulfill God's command. Contemplate these moving words about Isaac: "He tenderly seeks to lighten the father's grief, and encourages his nerveless hands to bind the cords that confine him to the altar" (*Patriarchs and Prophets,* p. 152). Moreover, "He was a *sharer* in Abraham's faith, and he felt that he was *honored* in being called to give his life as an offering to God" (ibid., emphasis supplied).

The Muslims' holy book, the Koran, describes God as declaring: "And We have ransomed him [Abraham's son] with a *tremendous Victim*" (37:105, emphasis supplied). The Muslims commemorate this important event by celebrating with the Feast of el Adha (sacrifice) and killing a sheep to symbolize Abraham's great sacrificial act of offering his son to God. It seems that the Koranic reference to the "tremendous Victim" provided by God had to be more than merely a sheep. Most likely it refers to God providing His own Son as that tremendous Sacrifice to redeem Isaac and humanity. Such tremendous redemption could not be obtained by the blood of animals but by the blood of the Son of God, who possesses life and can freely give it.

The Koran presents Christ as a *unique* person in comparison with any other prophet, including their own prophet Mohammed. Professors C. George Fry and James R. King state that "Christians are interested to learn of the high regard Muslims have for

Jesus. . . . Jesus, it is taught, was born of a virgin, without human father, and lived a sinless life. He is given titles of honor bestowed on no other prophet" (*Islam: A Survey of the Muslim Faith,* p. 60).

As already discussed earlier in this chapter, the Koran teaches the virgin birth of Jesus, the Son of Mary. It was a miraculous act of God upon Mary, without the involvement of a man. We also learned that this was referred to as a "sign" from God, just as Isaiah refers to it (see Isaiah 7:14).

It also gives Jesus the divine title "Word" from God. Listen to these words from Surah 3:45, "O Mary! God giveth thee Glad tidings of a Word from Him: His name will be Christ Jesus, the son of Mary." In Arabic the prepositions *of* and *from* refer to the same category or genre. Thus the expressions *Word from God,* and *Word of God* may mean the same thing. The Muslim scholar Muhyi Al Din Al Arabi explains that "the word is Allah [God] in theophany . . . and is the one divine person, not any other" (cited in Anis A. Shorrosh, *Islam Revealed,* p. 91). Also we find other Koranic references indicating the divinity of Jesus. One such reference specifically depicts Him as the "Word of God": "Isa [Jesus] bin Mariam Kalimat Allah," which means "Jesus, Son of Mary, Word of God" (Seamands, p. 229). Jesus is also referred to as the "Spirit of God" and as "Lord." He is spoken of as "Rabba na Isa." The Arabic word *Rabb* literally means "Lord." Thus the expression *Rabba na Isa* means "Our Lord Isa (Jesus)." And the word *Lord* in Arabic or the Islamic religion signifies supremacy and divinity.

Furthermore, according to Islamic teachings, Christ is one of the six most prominent prophets. Each one of these six is given a specific title, but Jesus is given the divine title of "the Word of God." Thomas Starkes, in his book *Islam and Eastern Religions* (p. 37), gives this list of the prophets with their appropriate titles:

Adam, the Chosen of God
Noah, the Preacher of God
Abraham, the Friend of God

Moses, the Speaker of God
Jesus, the Word of God
Mohammed, the Apostle of God.

In Middle Eastern or Semitic culture, a man is always called the son of his father unless his father is unknown; then he is called the son of his mother—hence, Jesus, "the son of Mary." The term *Word* was used by the Jews to point to the would-be coming Messiah. This term is the same as *Logos* in Greek, and was also used extensively by the Gentiles and the followers of Plato to denote divinity (see *Barnes' Notes on the Old and New Testaments: Luke and John,* p. 173).

Nanak, who was influenced by the Muslims in northern India, and who founded the Sikh religion in the latter part of the sixteenth century A.D., taught that God is ultimately the Creator of the world by "an emission of a Primal Utterance (Word, Logos)" (Noss and Noss, p. 239). This sounds strikingly close to what John wrote, doesn't it? "In the beginning was the Word, and the Word was with God, and the Word was God. . . . All things were made through Him, and without Him nothing was made that was made" (John 1:1, 3).

Finally, Jesus is called "the Spirit of God" (Ruh Allah) in the Koran (see Seamands, p. 204). He is considered sinless and perfect in righteousness. The angel of the Lord said to Mary: "I am only a messenger of thy Lord, that I may bestow on thee a faultless [holy] son" (Koran 19:19). And He will be the judge of the world at the end of time. The Hadith of Al-Bukhari quotes Mohammed as saying: "In the name of God who preserves my soul, verily Jesus, the son of Mary, will come soon as the righteous judge" (quoted in Wieland, p. 110). Some Shiite Muslims believe that the Mahdi (Messianic figure) who will come to judge the world is none other than Jesus. "There is no Mahdi but Jesus the Son of Mary" (Noss and Noss, p. 573).

The well-known archaeologist Siegfried Horn describes his visit to the Omayyad mosque, the most illustrious building in Damascus, Syria. A temple of Jupiter once stood there during the Roman Empire, and was later replaced by a large Christian cathedral dedicated to John the Baptist in A.D. 379. The Muslim Arabs took over Syria in the early part of the seventh century, and the Caliph Walid transformed this magnificent cathedral into a Muslim mosque in A.D. 705. However, with all the structural alterations, a Christian inscription in Greek was left preserved over the south gate of the mosque: "The kingdom, O Christ, is an everlasting kingdom; and thy rule lasts from generation to generation" (see *The Spade Confirms the Book,* pp. 291-293).

On several visits to this mosque as a youngster, I saw such a Greek inscription, but could not decipher its meaning. Although this cathedral has been used by Muslims for nearly thirteen hundred years, "this inscription, dating from the fourth century, has been allowed to remain where it was before the church was converted into a mosque. . . . [It] is still a silent but eloquent witness for the everlasting power of Christ's kingdom." Dr. Horn reported that he was informed by the local people that the square minaret at the southeastern corner of this Omayyad mosque is called the Minaret of Jesus. It is quite likely that the Muslims left this inscription intact because they "believe that Jesus will descend from heaven upon this minaret on the day of judgment to destroy the antichrist" (ibid., p. 293).

CHAPTER
5

The People Chosen

King David, the illustrious ancestor of Christ (see Luke 1:32), whom the prophet Samuel called a man after God's own heart (see 1 Samuel 13:14), felt keenly the intense desire to trade places with his dead son Absalom. This obstinate son fomented a national rebellion and was defiantly determined to fight it out with his father to the bitter end. And yet, Absalom's death resulted in this mighty king pacing the floor of his palace and through his bitter tears saying: "O my son Absalom—my son, my son Absalom—if only I had died in your place! O Absalom my son, my son!" (2 Samuel 18:33).

If David's heart convulsed in anguish over his wicked son, imagine how much more God's heart felt toward His perfect and only beloved Son. We might think that God suffered much less than His slain Son. But if that were not true of David, an earthly father, how could this ever be true of God, the heavenly Father? In a sense, our heavenly Father shared in the suffering and agony of the cruel cross and felt it as intensely, if not more, than His Son. The apostle Paul declares that "God was in Christ reconciling the world to Himself" (2 Corinthians 5:19).

The Father must have loved this lost world as much as He loved His Son to have been willing to accept Christ's voluntary sacrifice of Himself. That was God's eternal plan from the beginning: to let all the inhabitants of this world know that He would provide the Lamb to be sacrificed in their place. Therefore, in order to accomplish this eternal plan of redemption, He needed to find a godly person like Abraham through whom His Son could be incarnated.

As God surveyed the nations, searching for a righteous person to use, He discerned in Abraham such a suitable man. He chose this special friend not merely for his own sake and the sake of his immediate descendants, but for the sake of the entire world. In him God found the suitable person to set in motion His eternal plan to bring the Messiah into this world and share the good news of His universal salvation with all humanity.

That is why the Scriptures are full of references to God's consuming desire to bless all the nations of the earth through Abraham's seed. And in doing so, God again risked being misunderstood as a Father playing favorites among His children by favoring the Hebrew nation. With the privilege of being called to be God's messengers, the Hebrews also received proportionate and weighty responsibilities of living godly lives before Him and the world. The Hebrew people suffered greatly as a result of their recurrent disobedience to God and often presented a regrettable example before the world.

God's covenantal election of the children of Israel was by no means an end in itself. He was not, for some reason, inordinately obsessed with them for their own sake. But He elected them for the glorious purpose of blessing them with righteousness and consequently blessing His entire world through them. He did not love them more than the world; neither did He love the world less than Israel. He wanted to love the whole world through them. Divine election was not granted for its own sake but carried with it human responsibility.

Therefore, it "was for the purpose of bringing the best gifts of Heaven to *all the peoples of earth* that God called Abraham out of from his idolatrous kindred and bade him dwell in the land of Canaan" (*Prophets and Kings,* p. 15, emphasis supplied). Moreover, "it was God's purpose that by the revelation of His character through Israel men should be drawn unto Him. To *all the world* the *gospel* invitation was to be given. Through the teaching of the *sacrificial service, Christ was to be uplifted before the nations,* and all who would look unto Him should live" (ibid., p. 19, emphasis supplied).

In our discussion, it's important that appropriate emphasis is placed on God's perfect love, which embraces every human being, regardless. No one "has a corner on God," so to speak, for He loves each person the same and ardently desires all to be saved. There is absolutely no logical reason why God would love one human being more than another. He created them all in His image; hence, they are all His precious children. Though He selects some of them to reveal His unconditional love to His other children far away from home, this in no way proves any impartiality toward the one. On the contrary, it shows His stubborn love and solemn commitment to all of the others. One has only to think of Christ's parables of the lost coin, the lost sheep, and the prodigal son to clearly see how His love doggedly pursues the ones who strayed away from home. And when He notices that some of them are lost and away from home, His loving heart goes out to them. They are the ones who need the most help lest they perish, for He "desires all men to be saved and to come to the knowledge of the truth" (1 Timothy 2:4).

God chose to use Abraham and his descendants as a means of bringing His lost children home. Even among the chosen people themselves, it was impossible to use more than one tribe and one person to provide the promised sacrificial Lamb and to incarnate the Son of God. Undoubtedly, the line of Judah was not the only righteous one. But obviously only one righteous person (the virgin Mary) was needed in order that the eternal Word might become flesh and dwell among us (see John 1:14).

The very fact that such non-Israelites as Rahab and Ruth figured in the divine plan of becoming ancestors of the Messiah shows God is impartial toward one group of people as compared with another. Remember that Rahab was not only a Canaanite but a harlot, and Ruth was a Moabite. However, what really matters is that they turned away from idolatry to the worship of the true God.

In attempting to succinctly describe the three great monotheistic religions—Judaism, Christianity, and Islam—three key words come to mind. Judaism places its emphasis on God's *justice;* Christianity on God's *love;* and Islam on God's *power.* This does not say that all these attributes of God do not overlap or are not manifested in all these religions, but that each one of these religions of the descendants of Abraham emphasizes a specific attribute.

Philip Hitti, a renowned expert in Islamic history, explains that the Muslims ascribe to Allah (who is the same as the God of the Bible) "ninety-nine names and as many attributes. The full Moslem rosary has ninety-nine beads corresponding to His names." Then Hitti goes on to emphasize that God's "attributes of love are overshadowed by those of might and majesty" (*The Arabs,* pp. 47, 48).

However, special spiritual significance lies in the truth that pervades the Scriptures that "God is love" (1 John 4:8). The verb *is* conveys His eternal state of being. Love is the perfect reflection of His character and sweeps in its train His justice, power, and all of His other attributes. For, you see, justice without love culminates in despair, and power without love is tyranny.

In their emphasis on legalistic justice, the Jews, the descendants of Isaac, considered the sinful heathen as undeserving of God's plan of salvation. That was one of the reasons why they had a difficult time accepting Jesus' emphasis of universal salvation. They were expecting a Messiah who would come to execute His retributive justice, unmixed with mercy, on all their enemies. In their spiritual blindness, they just could not see how Jesus could forgive sinners, reach out to the heathen, and die for the sins of the entire human race.

On the other hand, the Muslim Arabs, the descendants of Ishmael, in their emphasis on God's power and great reverence for the perfect Jesus, have a difficult time accepting the fact that an all-powerful God would allow the perfect Jesus to suffer a shameful death on a Roman cross. God simply could not allow such a scandalous event to be perpetrated against Jesus, whom they call the Word of God.

George Vandeman raises the rhetorical question as to how these literal descendants of Abraham can "consider themselves God's chosen people through the *blood of Abraham* while rejecting the *blood of Christ*" (*Showdown at Armageddon*, p. 31, emphasis supplied). He further asserts that "*to suggest that this covenant* [of being chosen] *could be fulfilled without faith in the Messiah* [His blood atonement] *would be to deny the agreement God made with Abraham.*" Then he adds that "outside of faith in the Messiah, God's covenant cannot be fulfilled. We must nail that down and never forget it" (ibid., p. 25). Unless the descendants of Abraham accept the true Seed (the Messiah), they cease to be his true seed. "If you are Christ's, then you are Abraham's seed, and heirs according to the promise" (Galatians 3:29).

It is sad that these descendants of Isaac and Ishmael reject the sacrificial Lamb that was promised their father Abraham on Mount Moriah. Consequently, they are left with just the ram sacrifice, the symbol without the reality, which is totally inadequate to give life to any human being. The Muslims still sacrifice sheep during their Feast of Sacrifice (Id el-Adha) to commemorate the submissive and sacrificial spirit of their father Abraham. But what they ought to celebrate even more is the submissive spirit of Christ and His Father, who cooperated in providing lost humanity with the Lamb of God (Christ), the ultimate Sacrifice.

The rabbi scholar Morris N. Kertzer was asked to identify the chief areas of disagreement between Judaism and Christianity. He stated that the Jews "recognize Jesus as a child of God in the sense that we are all God's children . . . and that we are made in His image" (cited in Leo Rosten, ed., *Religions of America,* p. 144). Then Rabbi Kertzer goes on to delineate the three fundamental Christological doctrines which they reject: first, the *divinity* of Jesus; second, the *incarnation* of Jesus; and third, the vicarious *atonement* of Jesus.

Kertzer explains that God cannot become flesh, because He "is purely spiritual; He admits of no human attributes." Furthermore, he explains as to why the Jews reject the idea of salvation *through* Christ. "It is our belief that every man is responsible for his own salvation." Also, "no one can serve as an intermediary between man and God, even in a symbolic sense. We approach God—each man after his own fashion—without a mediator" (ibid., pp. 144, 145). In that sense, the Jew then becomes his own saviour, and he does that with a feeling of pride in that self-centered accomplishment.

But in the fallen state of humanity none can save himself. Indeed, every person desperately needs the incarnation, the atonement, and the mediation of Christ. The entire Old Testament is centered in and built around humanity's great hope of the substitutionary sacrifice and atonement of the Messiah. For the biggest problems of every human being are sin and death.

Of course, the children of Isaac have had ample opportunities to understand this, for it was clearly presented in the sanctuary services, the Messianic prophecies, and events in their history. But the children of Ishmael had less opportunity than their cousins to become acquainted with the substitutionary atonement of Christ.

As mentioned earlier, they could not accept that a powerful God would allow Jesus to be disgraced as a criminal and die such a shameful death at the hands of His enemies. They believe that it merely *appeared* that Christ was crucified, but in reality some other person was substituted for Him, and He Himself was raised up to

God to witness against His persecutors on the day of judgment.

According to the Koran the Jews boasted by saying: "We killed Christ Jesus the son of Mary, the Apostle of God." Then it goes on to refute this allegedly false claim. "But they killed him not, nor crucified him, but so it was made to appear to them. . . . Nay, God raised him up unto Himself; and God is exalted in power" (Koran 4:157-159). When the Muslim religion emerged on the world scene in the early part of the seventh century A.D., Christians (especially some sects) held various conflicting views regarding the nature of Christ, and questioned whether He actually did die.

Even though the Muslims do not accept that Jesus experienced the criminal's death on the cross, they acknowledge that God allowed or caused Him to die. But then God resurrected Him and caused Him to ascend to be with Him. The Koran says that both God and Jesus affirm this fact. "Allah [God] said 'Jesus, I will cause you to die and cause you to ascend to Me' " (Koran 3:54). Moreover, Jesus is quoted as saying this of Himself: "So peace be on me, the day I was born, the day that I die, and the day that I shall be raised up to life (again)!" (Koran 19:33).

The Koran seems to indicate that God in His wisdom allowed Jesus to die, and then He resurrected Him to life. Jesus, the Son of Mary, was that "tremendous Victim." The ram which God provided Abraham was a type of that "Victim," and of that "Ransom" found in Jesus, the Lamb of God. No one was substituted for the ram that God provided Abraham in order to ransom Isaac, and also no one could serve as an adequate substitute for the sacrifice of Jesus to ransom us.

Jesus did not die simply because the Jewish and Roman leaders decided not to spare His life. He Himself volunteered freely to die for lost humanity. He said this of Himself: "Therefore My Father loves Me, because I lay down My life that I may take it again. No one takes it from Me, but I lay it down of Myself" (John 10:17, 18).

During the times of Mohammed, the theological and ecclesiastical condition of the Christian church in the Dark Ages, which he was exposed to, were pathetic, to say the least. The church was not only promoting superstition, indulgences, and veneration of images, but it promoted Mary into a deity and called for her worship. Mohammed felt compelled to call his people away from superstitions, veneration of idols, and the worship of their familiar families of gods; and there in Christianity he found many such abominations. Mohammed was not in any way against Christ, but fought against a type of pagan Christianity emerging at that time.

The pertinent words Mahatma Gandhi is reported as having said to Christians—"Give me your Christ but take away your Christianity"—captures well Mohammed's sentiment in this connection. Mohammed and his followers could not accept the divine sonship of Christ, because He was presented in the context of a family of deities: God the Father, Mary the Mother Goddess (Mariolatry), and Jesus their Son God. No wonder Mohammed is quoted as inquiring of Jesus in utter dismay, "O Jesus, son of Mary! Didst thou say unto mankind: 'Take me and my mother for two gods beside God?' " (Mohammed Pickthall, *The Meaning of the Glorious Koran,* 5:116, cited by Oster, p. 25).

Arnold J. Toynbee, the famed British historian, went as far as condemning the church during the Dark Ages of giving in to the pagan Greek polytheism and idolatry, and crediting Islam with recovering their Father Abraham's faith in one God. He writes that "from this shameful betrayal of the revelation of the One true God, Islam had received the pure religion of Abraham. Between the Christian polytheists on the one side and the Hindu polytheists on the other there again shone the light of monotheism" (*Civilization on Trial,* p. 76).

Both Judaism and Islam passionately teach the doctrine of strict monotheism. They carry this idea which they have in common to an extreme, thereby not allowing for any possibility of monotheism in the Trinity—three Persons in *one* God. Both reject the idea of the Messiah being the divine Son of God because of their exaggerated fear of slipping into polytheism.

The greatest sin in Islam is the *shirk*, which in Arabic means "association," referring to the idolatry of admitting that anyone can share in God's divinity. The most important and most frequently repeated Muslim statement of faith is the *Shahadah*, which is the formula bearing witness to the absolute unity of the one God: "I testify that there is no God but God; and Mohammed is His messenger." The Koran states emphatically that "they do blaspheme who say: God is one of three in a Trinity: for there is no god except One God" (5:76). And "your God is One God: There is no god but He" (2:163).

This has the same ring to it as the Hebrew *Shema* (statement proclaiming the absolute unity and exclusiveness of one God) recorded in Deuteronomy 6:4: "Hear, O Israel: The Lord our God, the Lord is one!" The *Shema* is the most sacred saying in Judaism, just as the *Shahadah* is the most sacred in Islam. The eminent Rabbi Abraham Heschel said this in defense of monotheism: "Monotheism, to this day, is at variance with vulgar thinking; it is something against which popular instinct continues to rebel. Polytheism seems to be more compatible with emotional moods and imagination than uncompromising monotheism" (*Between God and Man,* p. 102). Of course, when Heschel refers to polytheism, he includes the Christians who believe in the divinity of Jesus and in the doctrine of the Trinity.

The perfect example of God's love revealed toward humanity is found in Christ's sacrifice on the cross. There we find how the God of love, in order to redeem mankind, brought justice and mercy together. In Christ, the infinite demands of God's justice were fulfilled, and on humanity His boundless generosity of mercy was bestowed. Thus God remains just, yet the justifier of every one who believes in Christ (see Romans 3:24-26).

Even Nanak, the founder of Sikhism, fought against the tradition of rampant ostracism and taught God's acceptance and love of all. Indeed one of his greatest accomplishments was manifested in breaking down the caste barriers against the untouchables in India, who were condemned to a long life of misery and rejection. He declared that God regards all human beings as precious in His sight regardless of race, caste, or religion. Moreover, His love is so great that He is capable of forgiving all sins or any accumulated bad karma (deeds).

In contemplating what was the best name to use in describing God, Nanak settled on "the Kindly One," emphasizing His all-inclusive love and mercy. In trying to understand the Hindu, Christian, and Muslim religions' views on God, he happily concluded: "If any name is to be used, let it be one like *Hari* (the Kindly), which is a good description of His character; *for His mercy is inexhaustible, His love greater than His undeviating justice*" (Noss and Noss, p. 238, emphasis supplied).

That is why it was imperative for the Jews to temper their emphasis on legalistic justice with God's all-embracing love. Because of God's election of them, they thought that they alone were His beloved and sole recipients of His grace to the exclusion of all others. They were so obsessed with this imagined exclusivity of God that it became the heart of their religion. They focused so excessively on themselves being the literal seed of Abraham that they lost sight of the ultimate purpose for their calling, which was to bless all the world through the Seed of Abraham.

But that is a risk God took. In choosing them as vehicles to reveal Himself to the world, He hoped to keep their minds on Him and His ideal. Unfortunately, however, the Jews focused so much on themselves as the special chosen vehicles that they forgot about the road they were supposed to travel in order to bring the light of truth to their neighbors. They became self-centered and oblivious to their high destiny to reach the world with God's saving knowledge.

The eminent Jewish scholar, Isidore Epstein, explained that the children of Israel "were deluding themselves when they imagined that they were God's favorites. . . . He was not the God of Israel only; He was a universal God with universal morality, and His special relation to Israel demanded that they should make the divine standards their own" (*Judaism,* p. 43).

It's a part of one's human nature to be selfish and to think that he is the center of all things. From the very beginning of their relations as brothers, the sons of Abraham very likely argued about who was God's chosen.

Can you imagine how Ishmael must have been infuriated by his younger sibling's claiming to be the favorite of his father to win the birthright, and with it the inheritance? Undoubtedly, Ishmael felt jealous and threatened by his younger brother from the time he was born. As Isaac grew to boyhood, it is quite possible that such jealousy intensified, and Ishmael considered him a pest, or a spoiled brat, as the older siblings say today. After thousands of years, the same attitudes still exist. Today Palestinians frequently refer to their cousin Israel as "America's spoiled child."

These special feelings relating to the Jews go beyond the confines of the Middle East. For some reason, the Jews have been admired, envied, loved, hated, and persecuted probably more than any other people in history. One might ask why such manifestations of extreme human sentiments exist. It has to do with the unique historical mission given to them by God, which was intended to bless the nations of the world. According to Rabbi Meyer Jais: "Yahweh Himself chose Israel to be a messianic and theophoric people, thus making them the object of hostility before the world and pagan peoples, long before the incarnation, long before the deicide" (cited by Doukhan, p. 34).

Such very old feelings do not simply go away with the passage of time—decades, centuries, and even thousand of years. *Newsweek* reported in its cover story about such new anti-Jewish fears in the Eastern-bloc countries. "The collapse of communism has allowed old hatreds to resurface throughout Eastern Europe and the Soviet Union. Five decades after the Holocaust began, anti-Semitism is returning on the fringes of political life. The challenge is to keep it on the fringes" ("The Long Shadow," *Newsweek* [May 7, 1990], p. 34).

Through no other people had God revealed so much of Himself. It overwhelms us to think that the God of the universe, from all the peoples of the world, became so intimately connected with one person, one tribe, and one people. And it is quite possible that the blessing of such relationship with God in their ancient history still lingers on. This may account for their great achievements in all fields of knowledge, and their unusual resilience and enduring legacy.

Rabbi educator Morris Kertzer explains that the Jewish prayer book emphasizes the love of learning as one of their principal tenets of faith. From the first century, the Jews strictly committed themselves to a system of compulsory education, including even the poor and the fatherless. Furthermore, they were acquainted with the psychology of education and how to make learning a pleasant experience for the child. "On the first day of school, youngsters were fed honey cakes shaped in the letters of the alphabet so that they would associate learning with sweetness" (Rosten, p. 143).

God's high ideal for His people was designed to make them the greatest nation and His showcase in blessing all other nations. The fulfillment of this ideal was to be the result of their cooperation with God. Such blessings included: first, holy character; second, vibrant health; third, excellent intellect; fourth, skill in agriculture and animal husbandry; fifth, superior craftsmanship; sixth, exceptional prosperity; and finally, national greatness (*SDA Bible Commentary*, vol. 4, pp. 27, 28).

However, these blessings were not to exclusively benefit Israel, but to become an attraction to the other nations. These blessings were to lead them to inquire about their source and the reasons behind them. Hence, such gifts from God were not to be selfishly hoarded, but were to be shared with all peoples. For only in sharing them with others around them would the Israelites keep and enhance them. "In His law God has made known the principles that underlie all true prosperity, both of nations and of individuals. . . . The blessings thus assured to Israel are, on the same conditions and in the *same* degree, assured to *every nation* and to *every individual* under the broad heavens" (*Prophets and Kings,* pp. 500, 501, emphasis supplied).

From all peoples on the face of the earth, God spoke to their prophets and revealed His character through their thoughts and words. He gave them the Ten Commandments and the holy Scriptures, the two most important documents the world has ever known. For many centuries, the Western world has been quite at home with the names and stories of the Bible, and its civilization was founded on the Judeo-Christian principles. "As it happens, the oldest, most widely known super story of Western civilization is the Bible: its stories, its characters, and its values constitute the main lens through which Western man looks at himself and at the world. The Jews—the ancient Israelites—are the main characters in this biblical super story" (Friedman, p. 428).

Christ's disciples, whom we revere, were all Jewish, and they were the ones whom God inspired to pen the New Testament. The apostle Paul, the champion of Christianity, was himself a Pharisee and a prominent member of the Sanhedrin. The fledgling Christian church was pioneered by Jews who accepted the Messiah and His gospel. "The church as a whole," writes Karl Barth, "still owes everything to those [the Jews] to whom it is indebted for everything" (Pinchas Lapide and Ulrich Luz, *Jesus in Two Perspectives,* p. 20).

But most amazing of all was that God gave His own divine and eternal son to be born a Jew of the Jews. In God's divine plan the Jews had become "the flesh and bone of the Messiah," as Bernard of Clairvaux put it (ibid., p. 12).

We must also remember that God pronounced a special blessing on Ishmael and his descendants. God declared to Abraham the following message concerning his son Ishmael: "As for Ishmael, I have heard you. Behold, I have blessed him, and will make him fruitful, and will multiply him exceedingly. He shall beget twelve princes, and I will make him a great nation" (Genesis 17:20).

The history of Ishmael's descendants proves that God was faithful in His promise of great blessing. Not only is their identity and cultural heritage still preserved, but during the Dark Ages, while the West was languishing in its darkest periods of ignorance, their advanced knowledge in many disciplines greatly enriched the world.

The descendants of Ishmael always stressed the importance of seeking knowledge, and their adoption of the Islamic religion (submission to God) even enhanced that coveting of learning. Muslims, from their childhood, commit to memory the familiar sayings of their prophet Mohammed regarding the primacy of scholastic enlightenment: "Seek knowledge even unto distant China," he urged. And "the ink of the scholar is more holy than the blood of the martyr," he exhorted his followers. The Muslims diligently traveled far and near on their crusade to pursue knowledge. History reveals that they were as committed to going after such knowledge as to advancing their holy war (jihad) of territorial acquisition.

Arab scholars were devouring great works of philosophy, such as the works of Aristotle, when Charlemagne and his aides were beginning to learn how to write their names (see Hitti, p. 5). It was the Arabs who invented the Arabic numerals from 0 to 9; they also invented algebra, which comes from the Arabic word *al-jabr* literally meaning "the reduction." Moreover, they developed spherical and plane trigonometry and geometry, and they advanced the sciences of astronomy, natural history, and medicine.

An impressive inscription over a gateway of a center of learning in Spain, dating back to the time of the Muslims there, reads: "The world is supported by four things only: the learning of the wise, the justice of the great, the prayers of the righteous and the valour of the brave" (ibid., p. 174). "The learning of the wise" Arab scholars greatly influenced Western thought. "The Arabic-speaking peoples were the main bearers of the torch of culture and civilization throughout the world, the medium through which ancient science and philosophy were recovered, supplemented and transmitted to make possible the renaissance of Western Europe" (ibid., p. 175).

In a few centuries, the Islamic forces moved from the desert of Arabia with a lightning speed and efficiency to take control of all the regions of the Middle East, North Africa, Spain, and parts of France and southern Europe. Later on, their forces were able to cross into Europe from the east, conquering large regions of eastern Europe, reaching the gates of Vienna, and pushing all the way to southern Italy, the Alpine passes, and even reaching the shores of Lake Geneva in Switzerland (see Denise Lardner Carmody and John Carmody, *Ways to the Center*, p. 357).

Spending a few years in the 1980s working and traveling in west and central Africa and the islands of the Indian Ocean, I was frequently astonished at how widespread Islam is in that region of the world. Once on a trip to Madagascar, our plane landed for refueling on one of the Comoro Islands in the Indian Ocean. And there I was surprised to see airport signs painted in the Arabic language. I also learned that the people there were Muslims. Not only was the continent of Africa influenced by Muslim expansion, but almost every continent in the world, including such countries as India, China, and the Soviet Union. Among world religions, Islam is the fastest growing, boasting at least 800 million adherents (see Theodore M. Ludwig, *The Sacred Paths*, p. 208).

Muslim wealth is generously used to advance their missionary activities worldwide. They look at the post-Christian West, shackled by secularism and pervaded with materialism, and become eager to bring their monotheistic religion there. In England, for example, the Muslims are buying up many huge church buildings, and for a huge price. Many of these old churches are attended only by a few Christian believers, and their upkeep becomes expensive. So when a hefty price is offered for their purchase, it becomes almost impossible not to be tantalized by the temptation to be relieved of the burden.

It is hard to believe that "today in England, the birthplace of Methodism, there are more Muslims than there are Methodists" (Seamands, p. 19). Moreover, "Islam is now considered the second largest religion in Europe. . . . And in 1976 the Islamic Council of Europe announced its aim of establishing a mosque of reasonable size in each major city in Europe" (ibid., p. 26). Since then, this ambitious goal has been nearly accomplished, with hundreds of beautiful mosques erected in nearly all parts of that continent.

Even though Muslims usually do not allow freedom of evangelistic activities to Christians, they do not hesitate to seize every opportunity in the West to zealously propagate their own religion. And they do that with total liberty, because the West allows religious freedom for all. The aggressiveness of the Muslim evangelistic thrust is demonstrated by the fact that Muslim centers have been "established in *every* major European and American city in the last fifteen years" (Shorrosh, p. 172). France may be considered a case in point. Anis Shorrosh continues by stating that "France had but one mosque in 1974. Now there are fifteen hundred" (ibid.).

The Muslims' evangelistic impetus is built on the fact that at the height of the Islamic power they failed to militarily hold on to, or completely dominate, Christian Europe. So they think that they have come upon a golden opportunity to win the West spiritually, especially since they view the so-called Christian West as spiritually bankrupt. They look with disbelief at our soaring crime rate, secularism, rampant immorality, and other social ills, and they endeavor to grasp this unprecedented opportunity in order to fill that spiritual vacuum.

It's possible that God will use the zealous evangelistic inroads of the Muslims to awaken the Christian West out of its spiritual apathy and hedonism, and prompt a return to Him in repentance in these last days. In this post-Christian era, many Westerners feel that Christianity no longer has any value for them. That is why they find themselves seeking spiritual meaning and fulfillment in secular humanism, the New Age, the occult, and oriental religions. It is not inconsistent with God's character, as revealed in the Scriptures, to use even a heathen nation so that He might chastise His wayward people. So why wouldn't He use God-fearing Muslims in our times to provoke the Christian world out of its spiritual indifference?

This is by no means inconceivable on His part, considering the Muslim challenge to Christian Europe more than five centuries ago. That fierce challenge not only contained apostasy and kept in check the widespread idolatry in the church during the Medieval period, but it also prevented the Holy Roman Empire in league with papal power from snuffing out the infant Protestant Reformation. Martin Luther himself declared that "to fight the [Muslim] Turks is to resist the judgment of God upon men's sins" (C. D. Vaughan, *Europe and the Turk,* p. 135, cited in Oster, p. 69).

Why so? Because at that crucial time in the history of the Holy Roman Empire, Emperor Charles V could not afford to be overly distracted by Martin Luther's protest. He worried about the potentially dangerous disunity that would have ensued among his ranks. After all, he thought, that was not the best time to put down internal dissent, for he needed to unite the empire against its common enemy, the Muslim Ottomans. At that time, the Muslims were heading toward the very doors of Vienna, having conquered Constantinople, the capital of the Byzantine Empire, in A.D. 1453.

Several hundred years earlier, in the first part of the eighth century A.D., after the Muslim forces swept over all of North Africa, they intended to take control of all Christian Europe. So in A.D. 711 the Muslim military commander Tariq bin Ziyad, at the head of seven thousand men, crossed the Strait of Gibraltar to southern Spain. This strait has proven to be a great strategic connecting link between the Atlantic Ocean and the Mediterranean Sea. The name *Gibraltar* comes from the two Arabic words, *Jabal* and *Tariq,* literally meaning the "Mount of Tariq."

A story tells of the legendary bravery of Tariq bin Ziyad, who landed with his men on the shores of southern Spain. After ordering his men to sink all the ships, he exhorted them, saying: "The sea is behind you and the enemy is before you, and the only thing left for you to do is to put your trust in Allah [God] and fight in His name." With that kind of faith and determination, the Muslims took over all of Spain and parts of France.

And they would have certainly gone on further in their conquest, except for Christian general Charles Martel the Hammerer, who defeated them at the Battle of Tours in A.D. 732. The protracted battle proved to be decisive in the history of Christian Europe. For without this crucial victory, all Europe might have come under the domination of Islam.

Now the apostate Christian religion and the Holy Roman Empire were enclosed from the west and from the east by Muslim forces. A map of the period shows us that this Muslim enclosure looks like an open pair of pliers squeezing the regions of the medieval church. Kenneth Oster describes this containment as the Muslim crescent (symbol of Islam) stretching from the other side of the Mediterranean and enclosing both sides of Europe between its tips. "This great protective crescent," he writes, "had inexorably been cast around the enemy of the Reformation" (*Islam Reconsidered*, p. 55). Moreover, he asserts that this "crescent, albeit unconscious of its cosmic role, nevertheless did prevent the papacy from enforcing its dogmas on the rest of the world" (ibid., p. 56).

Church historian C. Mervyn Maxwell gives credit to the Ottoman Turks for playing "a vital role in the success of the Protestant Reformation" (*God Cares*, vol. 2, p. 254). Shaken by the recent fall of Constantinople, one of the great citadels of Christianity, and not being able to wage both internal and external wars on the Protestants and Ottomans respectively, Charles V had to ignore the Protestant Reformation for the time being (see ibid., pp. 254, 255).

Ellen White, in discussing the Protestant Reformation in her book *The Great Controversy*, made this pertinent statement: "God's providence had held in check the forces that opposed the truth. Charles V was bent on crushing the Reformation, but often as he raised his hand to strike he had been forced to turn aside the blow. Again and again the immediate destruction of all who dared to oppose themselves to Rome appeared inevitable; but at the critical moment the armies of the Turk appeared on the Eastern frontier, or the king of France, or even the pope himself, jealous of the increasing greatness of the emperor, made war upon him; and thus, amid the strife and tumult of nations, the reformation had been left to strengthen and extend" (p. 197).

God's unseen hand was definitely working behind the scenes of history as the descendants of Abraham experienced religious and political upheavals. Martin Luther was again recapturing that faith of Abraham. That message of faith in what God desires to do for those who trust Him reached again across the centuries through the voice of the Reformation.

Abraham learned that a person is not saved by his or her own efforts, but by having a living faith in the Lamb that God provides. God was again attempting to reveal what the true gospel is through the political and religious interaction between the Protestants on the one hand, and the Muslims and Christians on the other hand. Thereby all parties would mutually benefit in learning more about God's plan of salvation for all humanity—the very same gospel He revealed to Abraham, and the same gospel He desired all His children, be they Muslims, Jews, or Christians, to experience.

CHAPTER
6

The Fruit of the Vineyard

Whenever I study Jesus' parable of the vineyard in Matthew 21, I'm reminded of my childhood experience of helping my father tend our terraced vineyard in a hilly village overlooking the beautiful Syrian coast of the Mediterranean. I helped in building hedges, terracing, planting, grafting, pruning, and harvesting. Throughout the year, we spent time preparing the vineyard and giving it every opportunity to produce a plentiful harvest. We lacked modern means to keep the harvested grapes fresh, so the summer season was the only time to enjoy them. Thus we looked forward to seeing the leaves bud and the blossoms open, indicating harvesttime was on its way.

Everything was done to ensure a good harvest, but then it was time to wait. And we did wait, but we often checked on the vineyard's progress to ensure everything was going well. When the small sour clusters of grapes appeared, we knew that the ripened harvest was just around the corner. Impatiently we would sample some of the sour grapes, which only heightened our anticipation of the ripened clusters of grapes we would see at the time of the harvest. And when harvesttime finally arrived, nothing was more exhilarating than to eat the sweet fruit right off the vine.

However, occasionally I would be surprised and disappointed when I didn't find any grapes on a vine. Running my hands through the rich foliage, I couldn't understand why no fruit could be found. For all appearances the vine was a fruitful one. It was particularly disappointing, especially because everything favorable to producing rich fruit was there. The year-long care was in vain.

On a minute scale, I can understand God's bitter disappointment with His people, who produced no fruit of righteousness. The landowner (God) likened them to the tenants of his vineyard (His people). He did everything a landowner does to ensure a good harvest. He planted a good vineyard, he set a protecting hedge around it, he optimistically dug a winepress in it, and he built a tower to watch over it. Then after doing all that was necessary for a vineyard, he leased it, entrusting it to tenants, and went to a far country (see Matthew 21:33-41).

Then the landowner waited until harvesttime. As was normally expected by any landowner who leased his vineyard at that time, he sent some of his servants so that they might receive fruit from the tenants. But they callously mistreated these servants. In fact, they beat one, stoned another, and murdered one of them. In his longsuffering, the landowner sent more servants, hoping that the evil tenants would show more respect to them. Unfortunately, they received the same treatment.

Such cruel abuse of the servants was totally unwarranted. What had their master done to deserve this? He had entrusted them with his good vineyard, possessing the potential of a great harvest. Despite the continuing mistreatment, the landowner did not want to give up yet. So he went to the extreme extent of risking the life of his son by sending him as a last resort, hoping that the tenants would at least show some respect to his own son.

But they showed even more contempt to his son, the heir. In killing him, they thought they could assure their claim to the inheritance by becoming the landowners themselves, not just the tenants. Their contempt to the rightful heir was so fierce that they felt he did not even deserve to die in his own vineyard. They killed him and cast him outside the walls of his rightful property.

What the evil tenants in this parable did so infuriated the Jewish leaders, they pronounced miserable death on them, and they recommended leasing the vineyard to other tenants who were trustworthy. Unwittingly, they pronounced judgment upon themselves. The words of their own lips condemned them. Jesus simply concurred with their judgment by declaring: "Therefore I say to you, the kingdom of God will be taken from you and given to a nation bearing the fruits of it" (verse 43).

This new nation represented by spiritual Israelis consisted of all people, Jews and Gentiles, who accept Christ as their Saviour and Lord, and through intimate connection with Him produce the spiritual fruit of His kingdom. The apostle Peter describes these new tenants in language reserved only for God's chosen people—these "who once were not a people but are now the people of God." Moreover, he tells them that they in Christ are "a chosen generation, a royal priesthood, a *holy nation*, His own special people" (1 Peter 2:9, 10, emphasis supplied). For parallel examples of this important parable, see Isaiah 5:1-7 (the basis for Jesus' parable); Mark 12:1-12; Luke 20:9-19.

Untiringly patient, Jesus, the great Teacher, made use of the most effective method of instruction (the parable) to reach the hardened hearts of the Jews. In using this method of teaching, which they respected, He hoped to give them the greatest incentive to repent. Till the very end, He longed by any means to save them! In *Christ's Object Lessons*, Ellen White discussed the reason why Jesus used parables with the Jewish leaders. "In parables He rebuked the hypocrisy and wicked works of those who occupied high positions, and in figurative language clothed truth of so cutting a character that had it been spoken in direct denunciation, they would not have listened to His words" (p. 22).

Along with the fig and olive trees, the grapevine is one of the most valued and characteristic plants in the coastal regions of the Middle East. No one who lives in that part of the world can imagine living without them. They even assume a spiritual value, signifying peace, prosperity, and security. For example, the grapevine was so interwoven with the Jewish history and theology that it came to represent God's people Israel. In Isaiah 5:7 God describes His people thus: "The *vineyard* of the Lord of hosts is *the house of Israel.*"

Built in the midst of the vineyard (see Isaiah 5:2), the tower in the parable represented the temple, or God's presence in the midst of His people. "And as the tower in the vineyard, God placed in the midst of the land His holy temple" (*Christ's Object Lessons*, p. 288).

Near to the place where Jesus spoke was the temple. Its entrance was beautifully decorated with a "vine of gold and silver, with green leaves and massive clusters of grapes executed by the most skillful artist. This design represented Israel as a prosperous vine" (*The Desire of Ages*, p. 575; see also Psalm 80:8-16; Jeremiah 2:21). Represented by the tower, the temple itself was a wonder to behold, especially after King Herod spent years of labor and great expense in beautifying it.

In describing the appearance of the temple, Jewish historian Josephus wrote that "the exterior of the building wanted [lacked] nothing that could astound either mind or eye. For, being covered on all sides with massive plates of gold, the sun was no sooner up than it radiated so fiery a flash that persons straining to look at it were compelled to avert their eyes, as from the solar rays. To approaching strangers it appeared from a distance like a snow-clad mountain; for all that was not overlaid with gold was of purest white" (cited in Maxwell, *God Cares*, vol. 2, p. 15).

What a magnificent attraction for the worship of the true God it was! It was a shining city on a hill for all to see and be drawn to. But what would all that glory accomplish for Israel if they were not right with their God? It was indeed hollow without the glory and presence of God filling the temples of their hearts. The prophet Hosea correctly describes wayward Israel as "an empty vine, he bringeth forth fruit unto himself" (10:1, KJV). They had taken God's generous blessings for granted for so long that they considered them ironclad guarantees no matter what they did. Their father Abraham was always cited as the basis for their presumptuous claim to such rigid guarantees and uncontested rights. This pride and presumption eventually led them to such a haughty condition that they even "defied earth and heaven to dispossess them of their rights" (*Christ's Object Lessons*, p. 294).

The "choicest vine" (Isaiah 5:2) represents God's careful selection of the children of Israel, whom God planted in the land of Canaan. In commenting on this expression, Gerhard Hasel explains that "what the Owner planted in his Vineyard was not just choice vine of a new kind, but one which was of a stock fully tested over a long period of time." Then he goes on to say that this reminds us of "the heroes of faith such as Abraham, Isaac, Jacob, and Joseph who were the patriarchal forefathers of the Israelites" ("The Song of the Vineyard," North American Division Bible Conference, 1974, p. 6).

God transplanted them from Egypt in order to plant them in Canaan, the crossroads of the nations. He purposely selected Canaan as an ideal location so they might share the fruit of the gospel with all the peoples around them. In alluding to Israel as that vine, David addresses God in Psalm 80:8, 9 by saying: "You have brought a vine out of Egypt; You have cast out the nations, and planted it. You prepared room for it, and caused it to take deep root, and it filled the land."

Furthermore, the "choicest vine" is a figurative type of Jesus, the real Seed of Abraham, who also was called out of Egypt. Matthew

2:15 applies the prophecy of Hosea 11:1 to Christ. "When Israel was a child, I loved him, and out of Egypt I called My son." Jesus refers to Himself as "the true vine" in John 15:1. And the reason why the Jewish nation failed to produce the expected fruits of the Spirit and to reflect God's character in their lives was that they separated themselves from the true vine. Jesus said, "As the branch cannot bear fruit of itself, unless it abides in the vine, neither can you, unless you abide in Me" (John 15:4).

To help them abide in Him, He gave them every advantage for their spiritual growth and fruitfulness. There was nothing more He could do; and He reasoned with His people, appealing to their judgment to tell Him if they thought anything was left undone. "What more could have been done to My vineyard that I have not done in it?" (Isaiah 5:4), He asks of His people. More than anything else, He wanted to see them become fruitful, for their sakes as well as that of the entire human race.

Doing the best He could to have a first-rate vineyard, the land-owner built a hedge around it to preserve all the special work which He had already accomplished. In tending our vineyard as a young boy, I saw that the stones gathered in clearing the land were used to build a wall around the vineyard. This helped preserve its rich soil from erosion and kept foxes and other marauding animals from plundering it. One side of the vineyard was hedged with a high row of prickly pear, one of the cactus species that grows sharp, barbed spines on large, flat, and oval stem joints. I used to think it provided better protection than a barbed-wire fence.

The hedge that the Lord built around His people symbolized His great love and concern for them, as expressed in the gift of His divine law. The Ten Commandments were the expression of the precepts of God's character of love and were given to Israel to safeguard them against the rampant evil of idolatry all around them. "To this people [Israel] were committed the oracles of God," Ellen White writes. "They were hedged about by the precepts of His law, the everlasting principles of truth, justice, and purity. Obedience to these principles was to be their protection, for it would save them from destroying themselves by sinful practices" (*Christ's Object Lessons*, pp. 287, 288). Moreover, such spiritual protection resulting from true obedience goes hand in hand with spiritual fruitfulness. For "in the spiritual as in the natural world, obedience to the laws of God is the condition of fruit bearing" (ibid., p. 305).

Building a winepress (usually a trough hollowed out of solid rock) indicated that everything was ready to reap a bounteous harvest. The Lord not only anticipated gathering plenty of eating grapes to enjoy, but also had high hopes to reap such an overabundance of grapes that a winepress would be needed to accommodate the bumper crop.

However, no matter how glorious God's ideal of us is and regardless of the great incentives He provides for us, we will not succeed unless we cooperate with Him. He not only showered His people with many blessings, He went to the extent of giving them Himself in giving His son. And in that ultimate act He hoped that they would be jolted into realizing and forsaking their sins. In that Gift all of heaven was poured out on them. God could do or give nothing more. He gave all. What more can a person give than Himself?

Jesus asked the Jewish leaders to suggest what the owner should do with the evil tenants. Without hesitation, they recommended two things to be done to them immediately: one, destroy them miserably; and two, lease his vineyard to other tenants who were trustworthy (see Matthew 21:41). Jesus was not as severe on the wrongdoers as they were on themselves. He concurred with their second suggestion, to lease the vineyard to other tenants, but not with the first, to miserably destroy them. He pointedly declared to them: "I say to you, the kingdom of God will be taken from you and given to a nation bearing the fruits of it" (verse 43).

But in His mercy He kept the door open for them to repent. Of course, they would no longer constitute God's special nation entrusted with blessing the world with the gospel, but each one of them would be welcomed to return to God through accepting the sacrifice of His Son. Thus, joining spiritual Israel meant joining true followers of Christ from all the nations of the earth.

Yet even as they unwittingly pronounced judgement on themselves by condemning the evil tenants, they conspired to do exactly what they so vehemently condemned. They conspired to kill the Son of God, and would crucify Him in just a few days. They understood that Jesus agreed with their judgment in singling them out as those represented by the wicked tenants. This ominous point was not lost on them. Instead of repenting, they were filled with revenge and determination to carry out their plan.

The Jewish leaders seemed to have forgotten that they were only tenants, not owners of the vineyard. God Himself is the sole Owner. The vineyard of His people belongs to Him, not to them. The background of this parable, found in Isaiah 5, clearly states that fact: "The vineyard of the Lord of hosts is the house of Israel" (verse 7). And in usurping that divine right, they were responsible for the nation's sin and ruin (see *Christ's Object Lessons,* p. 305).

The practice of leasing or renting a piece of land stipulated that the renters would tend the land, and at the end of the season they would pay either in money or in a specified portion of the crop. Being reared in that part of the world, I often witnessed such transactions of sharecropping. For the sharecroppers to withhold that portion of the crop belonging to the owner would have been totally inconceivable. That initial breach in the contract would have normally in itself forfeited their right to continue as tenants. But they would never think of doing that, particularly if the landowner was a good person who entrusted them with a well-cared-for farm or vineyard.

Although the heavenly Landowner "leased" the vineyard to the tenants, they betrayed His trust by acting as if He had virtually sold it to them, hence removing all His rights to His property. They arrogantly acted as if they were the rightful owners, even though "the Lord had instructed His people that He was the owner of the vineyard, and that all their possessions were given them in trust to be used for Him" (ibid., p. 292). The conceited Jewish leaders acted as if they "owned" the God-given privilege of being His people.

However, God did not easily give up on them. For "last of all," after they had rejected, abused, and killed His messengers, and after they spurned all His entreaties to them, He sent His own Son, hoping that they would at least pay attention to the rightful Heir. It was within God's right to terminate the covenant immediately after they abused His first messengers and refused to produce or share the fruit of the harvest. However, even when they started to kill His messengers, He still continued to appeal to them, culminating with the strongest appeal ever: His own Son.

In his commentary on the Owner's hopeful words that they would show respect to His son, Adam Clarke explains that God, in this ultimate and final generous act, would cause them to "reflect upon their conduct and blush for shame because of it" (*Clarke's Commentary,* vol. 5, p. 206). In their spiritual blindness, they showed no shame. They refused to acknowledge Christ or submit to His rightful authority over them. At that very moment, they were conspiring among themselves to destroy Him, fulfilling the prediction in Christ's parable. "When the vinedressers saw the son, they said among themselves, 'This is the heir. Come, let us kill him and seize his inheritance' " (Matthew 21:38). "Finally the son of the owner is put to death, on the assumption that with the heir of the owner gone, the tenants can claim the property by reason of their occupying it" (Charles M. Laymon, ed. *The Interpreter's One-Volume Commentary on the Bible,* p. 636).

Thus the Jewish leaders made their fatal choice of rejecting their only Saviour and hope. They did not want to submit to Christ to rule over them. Rather, they were filled with envy and feared His popularity and success. Even when the heathen Roman ruler Pilate, whom they despised, lamely tried to change their evil plan toward Him, they still insisted on carrying it out. "Release to us Barabbas!" (Luke 23:18), they cried out. "Let Him [Jesus] be crucified!" (Matthew 27:22). And when Pilate reminded them that Jesus was their king, they responded, "We have no king but Caesar" (John 19:15).

History has shown that it is difficult to be given a position of honor or privilege without becoming proud, self-centered, and self-sufficient. Indeed, without God it is impossible. God was always there to sustain the Jews, reminding them and pleading with them through various means, over hundreds of years. But through it all, they were obsessed with the seen inheritance and lost sight of the Heir.

The whole purpose of appointing the Jews as the seed of Abraham was to lead them to accept the promised Messiah, the true Seed of Abraham, and consequently become co-heirs with Him. In a spiritual sense, the descendants of the seed of Abraham are dead without being born again of the incorruptible Seed of Christ (see 1 Peter 1:18-23).

In league with Satan, the Jewish leaders were doing all they could to thwart Christ's mission at every turn. Finally, they killed Him, hoping that they would forever get rid of Him and do as they pleased with His world. They wanted to keep Him in the tomb; when He was resurrected, they denied it and tried by all means to conceal it.

Yet in His very death, Christ guaranteed salvation for those who rejected and killed Him! He bought back fallen humanity with his priceless blood, so that "whoever believes in Him should not perish but have everlasting life" (John 3:16). Even as the blood of Christ was being spilled on the cross, His heart went out in forgiveness to His tormentors, and He actually appealed to His Father in their behalf. "Father, forgive them," He uttered, "for they do not know what they do" (Luke 23:34).

In the Messianic prophecy of Zechariah 13:6, Jesus even calls those who wounded Him "my friends." In a previous book, *Portraits of the Messiah,* the author writes thus in this connection: "It is astounding that Christ calls these whose hands were stained with His blood, 'My friends!' This innocent blood of Christ does not cry out in vengeance over those who spilled it. His blood flows as a continuous stream of forgiveness and love. The wounded hands are not clenched defiantly, but are stretched forth to embrace us in reconciliation" (Samaan, p. 118).

Of course, the Jewish leaders in cooperation with the Roman authorities knew what they were doing. However, they did not realize what implications their actions would have in the context of the universal struggle between good and evil. This amazing demonstration of Christ's altruistic divine character was totally opposite to the pride and selfishness of His crucifiers.

In a sense God gave them the benefit of the doubt so that somehow their conscience would be pricked. In fact, after hearing Peter's sermon in Acts 2, some of them "were cut to the heart" in repentance and joined the early Christian church (see verses 37-41). In the mystery of God's divine plan to redeem fallen humanity, the very shedding of Christ's blood outside the walls of Jerusalem worked as the only basis for the salvation of the human race, Jews or otherwise.

The Jewish nation rendered no fruit of the vineyard to God (see Matthew 21:34-39); and in Isaiah 5:2 it is stated that it "brought forth wild grapes." Regrettably, instead of bringing forth the sweet and nourishing fruits of the Spirit, they brought forth the rotten and debilitating fruits of their own rebellious spirit.

"The Jews based their hope of salvation on the fact of their connection with Israel. But Jesus says, I am the real Vine. Think not that through a connection with Israel you may become partakers of the life of God, and inheritors of His promise. Through Me alone is spiritual life received" (*The Desire of Ages,* p. 675). The fruit of the vine symbolized Christ's precious blood shed on Calvary. And we can be fruitful only as we accept His shed blood to cleanse us (for our righteousness is like filthy rags), and to give us life (for we are dead in sin) in union with Him.

Everyone desperately needs that connection with the living Vine. "The connection of the branch with the vine, [Jesus] said, represents the relation you are to sustain to Me. The scion is engrafted into the living vine, and fiber by fiber, vein by vein, it grows into the vine stock. The life of the vine becomes the life of the branch. So the soul dead in trespasses and sins receives life through connection with Christ" (ibid.).

If we are mere consumers of God's gifts, then we will become consumed in our selfishness. The Jews of old became so lost in words, ceremonies, and pride in their privileges and accomplishments that they did not discern the Son of God. They minored in majors and majored in minors. They became greater slaves to their own self-centeredness than when they were slaves in Egypt. Are we likewise slaves to our own selfishness, status, accomplishments, and spiritual apathy?

We live in a world which, for the most part, has rejected Jesus. Even when "He came to His own, . . . His own did not receive Him" (John 1:11). The crucial question to each one of us is: What have *we* done with Jesus? Have we truly received Him in our lives, or have we rejected Him? Paul admonishes us not to be boastful or haughty, because God had rejected the Jewish nation. "If God did not spare the natural branches, He may not spare you either" (Romans 11:21) because of unbelief. Do we have a vibrant and living communion with Him? Are we revealing His character in our lives for all to see?

May we, through Christ, be the true children of Abraham, the friend of God, following in his footsteps of faith. May we be born of Christ's incorruptible Seed, bringing forth abundant fruit. And may these words of John be a vivid reality in our daily lives. "As many as received Him, to them He gave the right to become children of God, even to those who believe in His name: who were born, not of blood, nor of the will of the flesh, nor of the will of man, but of God" (John 1:12, 13).

CHAPTER
7

The Remnant of the Seed

The people of Israel were not only represented by the grapevine, as we have seen in the previous chapter, but also by the figure of the olive tree. These two hardy plants are often associated with each other in the Scriptures, and both signify positive qualities such as vitality, fruitfulness, peace, and prosperity. In Bible lands the olive tree has been considered extremely valuable: its fruit was both an essential commodity and a staple in the diet of the peoples of the region. It yields a rich harvest with a minimum of care. One olive tree may yield many gallons of oil.

Considered a sacred symbol used in the kings' anointing of consecration (see 2 Kings 9:6), this golden oil also represented the Holy Spirit (see Zechariah 4:3-6). Moreover, this oil was utilized in many useful ways, including cooking, lighting, and healing. The apostle James associates olive oil with healing, for he instructed the Christian believers to use it in anointing the sick and praying for them (see James 5:14). And the Good Samaritan in Christ's parable used this oil to treat the wounded man (see Luke 10:34). When I was a child, my parents used olive oil to treat my minor cuts and bruises. They picked the ripe, dark fruit and squeezed its fresh oil on the wound. That usually took care of the problem.

The apostle Paul uses the olive tree to depict the experience of the people of Israel, and how they were to provide spiritual nourishment, light, and healing to the world. God planted Israel as a good and beautiful olive tree in the land of Canaan. He desired to see it anchor its deep roots in the soil and to spread its branches wide. He patiently waited to see His good planting diffuse His blessings among the nations and illumine the world with the light of His saving knowledge.

Tragically, however, His loving care and long-suffering went unheeded to a great degree. For hundreds of years, He waited to see the fruitfulness of His people bless the nations, but to no avail. In many ways they failed at emulating their symbol of the olive tree sharing its rich blessings with others. Instead, they selfishly hoarded such blessings to themselves, and that proved their undoing.

The fine qualities of this sturdy and productive tree also served as a valuable object lesson to the children of Israel and a constant reminder of God's divine plan for them. With all these powerful reminders, why didn't the ancient nation of Israel succeed in fulfilling God's divine plan of salvation for humanity? Did they become so attached to what is temporary, to their heritage and national exclusiveness, that they detached themselves from the living connection with their God? There is no possibility that tree branches can remain alive without a living connection with the trunk.

I learned this important lesson assisting my father in grafting olive trees in our orchard. We would take cultivated olive shoots, make incisions in the natural or wild trees, and then proceed to graft them in, tightly wrapping them together. One time, as we were inspecting how the grafted branches were progressing, one olive shoot was noticeably dry. Upon closer observation, we discovered that the grafted shoot was loose and separated from the tree.

Romans 11 employs this symbol of the olive tree to illustrate how some of its branches were broken off and how some others were grafted in their place. However, in Paul's example, this grafting procedure was reversed. Instead of the normal process of grafting cultivated shoots into a wild tree, it was rather the grafting of wild branches into a cultivated tree. Such reversion is appropriate, because literal Israel could be compared to a cultivated tree resulting from all the spiritual blessings God had bestowed upon it. And the Gentiles could be united to the faithful Israel of God and consequently become partakers of the same blessings of His divine covenant.

In discussing the vital subject of the covenant, one hears several adjectives used to describe it, such as *first, second, old,* and *new.* But we must keep in mind that basically "the provisions, conditions, and objectives of the 2 covenants are identical" (*SDA Bible Dictionary,* p. 243). Both covenants were eternal and unchangeable, because they were founded on God's initiative of giving His Son to save the world. And the same human response of appropriating such good news and sharing it with others was expected. "The new covenant, then, is nothing less than salvation by grace through faith, the reception of God's Spirit, enabling one to walk in newness of life. This is the New Testament gospel in *the heart* of the Old Testament" (*Seventh-day Adventists Answer Questions on Doctrines,* p. 222, emphasis supplied).

In the case of the old covenant, which was made with the children of Israel, they were called by God to experience the gospel themselves and also to share it with the nations around them. But when they failed to fulfill their part of the covenant, and when they sealed such failure with the rejection of the Messiah, God allowed the old covenant to evolve into the new one. God did not fail in this bilateral relationship with literal Israel, nor did His eternal covenant. For He was always faithful to the agreement and did His utmost to encourage them to reciprocate, but He would never force their will.

Consequently, it became impossible for Him to use unfaithful Israel to reach out to the nations with the gospel. After all, that was why He chose them in the first place, not just for their own sake, but for the sake of redeeming the fallen world. God simply had to act to bring about this change of expanding the mission of the covenant to include all His true followers from all corners of the earth. You see, everything about God's eternal covenant with His people was certain and reliable except for His people. That was the risky factor in the covenant, because they had the freedom to accept or reject its obligations upon them. In other words, God's eternal covenant does not change, *but people do.*

Therefore, He is not willing to stand still while the world goes to eternal ruin, but He is indeed willing to try different means in order to accomplish His same eternal purposes. He can do this and still remain perfectly faithful to the covenant. But the human race is too precious for Him not to try another way to fulfill His covenant.

Even His covenant with the Jews has not been changed as far as their own spiritual salvation is concerned. They are saved today exactly on the same basis as they were saved before—through God's grace revealed in the promised Redeemer. However, the Jews who do accept the Messiah are no longer the exclusive agents of the gospel to the world, but they share such privilege and responsibility by joining the universal members of spiritual Israel, or the Christian church. Hence there is to be found this spiritual unity and continuity of God's covenant of literal Israel and spiritual Israel.

The unfaithful Jews, in their pride and exclusiveness, were not accepting such important responsibility, and neither were they allowing others to accept it. Their lives resembled the barren fig tree, impressive in appearance, yet without fruit. They were wasting God's opportunities of reaching the world with the gospel by not being spiritually fruitful. They were also wasting the precious means by which He could use others to accomplish His mission.

Yes, Israel was the elect people of God. But that election was never meant to be automatic. It was conditional and primarily for the purpose of spreading God's knowledge of salvation. An automatic election, based purely on being literal descendants of Abraham, would definitely have undermined God's sovereignty. It would tie God's hands, so to speak, so that He would not be free to do what needs to be done to accomplish His eternal purposes. That cannot be allowed, for the eternal destiny of the world would then become hostage to such a mechanical and robotistic idea.

Jerry Gladson correctly argues that God simply cannot force His salvation irrespective of human response. "Scripture does not teach an irrevocable salvation," he explains, "whether of a nation or of an individual." And Israel's lack of response to God's plan was the reason why He "had no other choice but to carry out His purpose through others, and so brought into existence the Christian church as 'spiritual Israel' for the fulfillment of His purposes" ("Israel's Failure to Fulfill God's Purpose," *Review and Herald* [November 4, 1976], p. 7).

The distinguished scholar Rabbi Samuel Sandmel, in his lectures given at Duke University, pondered this question at hand: "Who is the elect of God? Is a people so by birth? Is a people so innately, automatically? If that is what election means, I for one cannot accept it. Indeed, in such a sense I must say that we, you and I, are not the elect of God. In such a sense no people is. When you and I make this recognition, we do not lower our status, but, rather, we aggrandize it." Then Rabbi Sandmel refers to the Jewish sage Hillel, who taught that "it is our arrogance which demeans us, and our humbleness which elevates us" (*The Several Israels,* pp. 105, 106).

God's election of Israel may be summed up in two important aspects. One was based on His divine love, grace, and faithfulness, and never on Israel's deserving such special treatment. There was nothing about the enslaved Hebrews that recommended them to God. He did not single out these freed Hebrews to be His peculiar people because they were more impressive than other nations. In fact, through Moses He said that they "were *the least of all peoples*" (Deuteronomy 7:7, emphasis supplied). Nor were they favored because they were distinguished for their righteousness, for they were a stubborn bunch (see Deuteronomy 9:6). God assured them that He would keep "covenant and mercy for a thousand generations," but on the important condition that they too would "love Him and keep His commandments" (Deuteronomy 7:9, 10; see also Richard Rice, *The Reign of God,* p. 186).

The second important aspect of Israel's election related to the special *purpose* for such an election. God, in His loving concern for all peoples, needed to use them to disseminate the knowledge of His plan of salvation to all. Richard Rice explains that "God was not playing favorites when He chose Israel; He did not intend to set them apart from other people as the exclusive objects of His love. . . . God didn't love Israel *instead* of the other people; He wanted to love all people *through* Israel. Israel was called to service, not elevated to a privileged status" (ibid., emphasis supplied).

Frank Holbrook gives adequate biblical support for universalism in Israel's mission, and not just particularism. He cites the prophet Ezekiel, for example, in showing that God purposely placed the Hebrews on the land bridge of Palestine, in the center of the three continents of Asia, Africa, and Europe. God said of Jerusalem, "I have set her in the *midst* of the nations and the countries all around her" (Ezekiel 5:5) for the purpose of effectively evangelizing the world (see *The Enigma of Israel,* p. 16).

Holbrook goes on to emphasize that "the religion that Israel had in trust from God contained nothing exclusive, nothing limited to one small group of people." Then he admonishes us that "we must never think of the insights about God and His will expressed in the Ten Commandments or the principles of the gospel as taught in the sacrificial system as 'Jewish,' as though they had no application to the entire world" (ibid., p. 18).

From among other biblical references, Holbrook appeals to the great hope God expressed through His prophet Zechariah toward the returned exiles. " 'Yes, many peoples and strong nations shall come to seek the Lord of hosts in Jerusalem, and to pray before the Lord.' . . . 'In those days ten men from every language of the nations shall grasp the sleeve of a Jewish man, saying, "Let us go with you, for we have heard that God is with you" ' " (Zechariah 8:22, 23).

The attitude of God toward literal Israel applies to spiritual Israel. His election of the Christian church was also clearly based on His unmerited love, grace, and faithfulness. Moreover, He has the same expectations of Christians, wanting them to reciprocate His love by demonstrating and sharing the gospel with the world. Paul addressed both Jewish and Gentile members of this Christian church when he wrote to them: "You see your calling, brethren, that not many wise according to the flesh, not many mighty, nor many noble, are called" (1 Corinthians 1:26).

Through this divine plan, a faithful remnant was always to be active in permeating the earth with God's true knowledge. And the good news is that there was never a time throughout human history when God did not have such a faithful remnant.

Furthermore, maintaining a faithful remnant for the purpose of reaching the entire world was not intended for our world only. In our own shortsighted and self-centered way, we often try to limit His divine plan for the whole universe. Often we feel that who we are and where we are is the center of God's vast universe. He is not only the Creator of our world, but also of beings in other worlds of His universe. Therefore, by calling us to be His loyal remnant, He, first of all, wants to save us. Then, second, He wants us to spread His saving knowledge in all the world. Third, God endeavors to silence Satan's false accusations against Him and His eternal plan of salvation. And finally, He desires through His true remnant to demonstrate to all the unfallen beings in the other worlds of His creation the truth about His love and character.

The two main characters in this book, Father Abraham and his Seed, the Messiah, were certainly involved in this universal struggle and salvation. Abraham, a faithful remnant from the Chaldees, was probably accused by Satan before the angels of not being faithful to the covenant. So God wanted to demonstrate before the universe the faith and trustworthiness of His servant by asking him to sacrifice his only son Isaac, and at the same time reveal more clearly His eternal plan of salvation to the universe.

The unfallen beings had found it difficult to fully comprehend the mystery of salvation to be wrought in the death of their beloved Commander, the very Son of God. But as they witnessed the faith and submission of Abraham and his son, who were tested and vindicated, and as they witnessed God confirming His covenant with a solemn oath, "light was shed upon the mystery of redemption, and even the angels understood more clearly the wonderful provision that God had made for man's salvation. 1 Peter 1:12" (*Patriarchs and Prophets,* p. 155).

Moreover, many hundreds of years later, Christ, the antitype of Isaac, submitted Himself to the wrath of His Father's justice, and thereby sealed the eternal covenant with His own spilled blood. And the completion of this work of redemption was not only greatly significant for us, but also for the angels and the unfallen worlds. The angels "with us share the fruits of Christ's victory" (*The Desire of Ages,* p. 758).

But the profound faith of Abraham and the trusting submission of Isaac were not just a reflection of their characters, but more so, a reflection of God's enduring love and His absolute trustworthiness. Just as the success of one's students is a reflection on the quality of a teacher, so also our spiritual success is a reflection on God's character.

In describing the survival of this remnant against various odds, Gerhard F. Hasel, who researched the biblical motif of the remnant, argues that such survival is based solely on a vital connection with God. "Ultimate survival, the deepest securing of one's existence, and the most satisfying inner experience comes on *one basis alone* and that is a whole-hearted and complete return to God in letting Him be the Lord of all one's longings, desires, and hopes" (*The*

Remnant, p. 403, emphasis supplied).

Israel as a nation has been repeatedly unwilling to submit itself to its only source of life and destiny: their promised Messiah. For more than a thousand years God patiently waited to accomplish His divine will through them. In their self-centeredness and spiritual blindness, they somehow interpreted His promises as centered completely on the nation of Israel, and not on the promised Saviour, for whose incarnation and gospel the whole nation of Israel came into being.

"Bible scholars are now beginning to recognize more and more the fact that the Old Testament as a whole is not primarily Israel-centered, but *Messiah-centered*," Hans K. LaRondelle writes. "The heart of Israel's prophetic and historic mission is the Christ. This implies that we can understand the prophecies of the Bible properly only when we relate the prediction to God and to His Messiah, the anointed Son of God (see 2 Corinthians 1:20)" (*Chariots of Salvation,* pp. 23, 24).

Moreover, "in every page, whether history, or precept, or prophecy, the Old Testament Scriptures are irradiated with the glory of the Son of God. So far as it was of divine institution, the entire system of Judaism was a *compacted prophecy* of the gospel" (*The Desire of Ages,* p. 211, emphasis supplied). The self-centeredness of the Jewish leaders led them to interpret the Messianic prophecies to foster their temporal ambitions.

This selfish approach did not cause them to earnestly humble themselves and search their hearts in genuine repentance in order to be right with God. "They did not seek redemption from sin, but deliverance from the Romans" (ibid., p. 30). And they did not want the promised Messiah to rule in their hearts, but to rule over their enemies. In their minds, the eternal plan of God was reduced to subjugating another nation, instead of calling for them to be heralds of salvation to all nations.

Israel as a nation rejected the Messiah, but not all individual Jews followed suit. As Paul states, *some* of the branches of the olive tree

BLOOD BROTHERS

were broken off, indicating that others were not broken off. The Jews who accepted Jesus as their Messiah, including, of course, His disciples, were the ones who remained connected to the olive tree. This faithful remnant was a culmination of an ever-existing faithful remnant throughout Jewish history.

In Romans Paul refers to one of these faithful remnants, the seven thousand during the time of Elijah. Discouraged, the prophet actually thought that he was the only one who remained faithful, but God gently said to him: "I have reserved for Myself seven thousand men who have not bowed the knee to Baal" (Romans 11:4). In a sense, God's divine purpose for the Jews had not entirely failed. Himself a Jew, the apostle Paul, along with Christ's Jewish disciples and all the other Jews who accepted Christ, demonstrates this fact.

Throughout history there has always been a faithful remnant, no matter how bleak or hopeless the situation seemed to be. Paul confirms this when he writes that "at this present time there is a remnant according to the election of grace" (Romans 11:5). Ellen White describes them this way: "Notwithstanding Israel's failure as a nation, there remained among them a goodly remnant of such as should be saved. At the time of the Saviour's advent there were faithful men and women who had received with gladness the message of John the Baptist, and had thus been led to study anew the prophecies concerning the Messiah. When the early Christian church was founded, it was composed of these faithful Jews who recognized Jesus of Nazareth as the one for whose advent they had been longing" (*The Acts of the Apostles,* pp. 376, 377).

Even during times of apostasy and exile, and reaching all the way to the time of Christ, a remnant of literal Israelites existed, faithfully serving God. Paul refers to such as true Jews, who experienced the inward circumcision of the heart. In this sense, then, not all Jews belong to the true Israel. He explains: "He is not a Jew who is one outwardly, nor is that circumcision which is outward in the flesh; but he is a Jew who is one inwardly, and circumcision is that of the heart, in the Spirit, and not in the letter; whose praise is not from men but from God" (Romans 2:28, 29). And Paul belonged to such true circumcision with all the faithful ones "who worship God in the Spirit, rejoice in Christ Jesus, and have no confidence in the flesh" (Philippians 3:3).

The Jewish Talmud teaches that "a single Israelite is worth more before God than all the people who have ever been or who shall be. They considered this connection a substitute for the repentance and good works for which John and Jesus called" (*SDA Bible Commentary,* vol. 5, p. 299). Their dangerous delusion lay in flattering themselves and conceitedly presuming that they could well substitute their physical lineage with Abraham for a life of faith.

According to Jesus, the genuine descendants of Abraham were characterized not by the blood of Abraham, but by the faith of Abraham—that spiritual relationship we have with him through faith in the Messiah (see John 8:39-44). Jesus also emphasized that "*whoever* does the will of My Father . . . is My brother and sister and mother" (Matthew 12:50, emphasis supplied).

The Jews' hardened attitude prompted John the Baptist to tell them that the sovereign God is not limited in finding faithful children. He would not slavishly tolerate the rebellion of the Jewish leaders simply because they claimed the right physical ancestors. Not only can God find for Himself new children of Abraham from among Gentile people, but He can even create for Himself such children of Abraham out of common stones. John said, "Do not think to say to yourselves, 'We have Abraham as our father.' For I say to you that God is able to raise up children to Abraham from these stones" (Matthew 3:9).

God is mainly interested in the faithfulness of people, who, in turn, help others to be faithful to Him as well. Paul appeals to the prophecy in Isaiah 10:22 that "though the number of the children of Israel be as the sand of the sea, the remnant will be saved" (Romans 9:27). He also refers to this saved remnant of Israel as a "seed," which God preserved from destruction (see Romans 9:29).

This prophecy quoted by Paul comes from Isaiah 1:9, where the term used for *seed* is a *small remnant.* And without this faithful remnant in Israel, the rejection of Israel would likely have been as complete as the destruction of Sodom and Gomorrah.

This unbroken line of the small yet faithful remnant continued till Christ's time and was joined by the believing remnant from the Gentiles. In this connection, Paul applies the prophecy in Hosea 2:23 to the converted Gentiles: " 'I will call them My people, who were not My people, and her beloved, who was not beloved.' 'And it shall come to pass in the place where it was said to them, "You are not My people," there they will be called sons of the living God' " (Romans 9:25, 26).

Indeed, throughout human history, "never has the Lord been without true representatives on this earth who have made His interests their own. These witnesses for God are numbered among the spiritual Israel, and to them will be fulfilled all the covenant promises made by Jehovah to His ancient people" (*Prophets and Kings,* p. 714).

Such a remnant of believing Jews and Gentiles are described by the apostle Paul: "At this present time there is a remnant according to the election of grace" (Romans 11:5). And in this believing remnant, "there is neither Jew nor Greek, there is neither slave nor free, there is neither male or female; for you are all one in Christ Jesus. And if you are Christ's, then you are Abraham's seed, and heirs according to the promise" (Galatians 3:28, 29).

This faithful remnant does not by any means constitute an unchangeable special group. Rather, God's grace as well as His judgment keep things open and flexible. Regardless of who is involved, the fact remains that those who are faithful He will honor, and those who are not, He will chastise. According to Romans 11:22, 23 not only can the branches that were cut off be grafted back in again, but also the ones grafted in can be broken off.

Lest we think that Jesus gave up on the Jewish nation too easily, let us consider the following: Even though He rejected them as His nation, or His theocracy, He did not reject them as individuals. And He did not reject the theocracy established with literal Israel without providing for them and all believers another vehicle to accomplish His will. That vehicle is His church, or spiritual Israel. In all His ministry Christ emphasized His first priority: to reach the Jews with the gospel.

Remember what He told the Syro-Phoenician woman to test her faith in Him: "I was not sent except to the lost sheep of the house of Israel" (Matthew 15:24). And in sending His disciples on their first missionary journey, He made sure that they would go first to "the lost sheep of the house of Israel" (Matthew 10:6). And even up to the time of His Ascension, when He gave His disciples the great commission to evangelize the world, His words implied that they start with the Jews first.

The following moving excerpts from the pen of Ellen White convey some of the depth of feeling Jesus held toward His wayward people shortly before they were to crucify Him. The multitude following Him witnessed with astonishment "His body rock to and fro like a tree before the tempest, while a wail of anguish bursts from His quivering lips, as if from the depths of a broken heart" (*The Desire of Ages,* p. 575). "It was the sight of Jerusalem that pierced the heart of Jesus. . . . He had come to save her; how could He give her up?" And "Jerusalem had been the child of His care, and as a tender father mourns over a wayward son, so Jesus wept over the beloved city. How can I give thee up? How can I see thee devoted to destruction?" (ibid., pp. 576-578).

Obviously Israel as a nation, as a theocracy, did not accept the long-awaited Messiah, but a believing and witnessing remnant vibrantly emerged from the ruins of their house, which was left to them desolate (see Matthew 23:38). The twelve apostles from Jewish stock constituted Christ's "little flock" (see Luke 12:32; Isaiah 40:11). These twelve from the stock of Israel, to whom Christ promised His kingdom (see Luke 22:29), were the founders of spiritual Israel, just as the twelve patriarchs were the founders of ancient

Israel. Later Christ chose seventy more disciples, also from among the Jews, apparently to correspond to the seventy elders appointed by Moses in ancient Israel (see Luke 10:1; Numbers 11:16).

Even today we might be tempted to think that only certain individuals or groups belong to this remnant. This might be so because we often look at the outward appearance, but God looks at the heart. As His eyes run back and forth across the earth, He knows well the ones who are His. No matter what background a person comes from, the crucial criteria for belonging to this remnant is to truly know Christ and to live for Him.

In an editorial entitled "A String of Surprises," Kit Watts describes how startled those were who thought they would have a seat reserved for them at the Messianic feast, only to discover that such seats would be given to total strangers. "Today, we also eat and drink with Jesus," she writes. "We listen to His Word from our pulpits. . . . We are *familiar* with Jesus, but have we come to *know* him?" Then she ponders this challenging question: "Is it possible that people from less-favored backgrounds may ultimately come to respond more wholeheartedly to God than we?" (*Adventist Review* [June 14, 1990], p. 5).

This new and faithful remnant from all the world is not a *replacement* of Israel but a *continuation* of the ever-existing genuine remnant of Israel. Hans LaRondelle explains that "Christ created His Church, not *beside* Israel, but *as* the faithful remnant of Israel that inherits the covenant promises and responsibilities" (*The Israel of God in Prophecy,* p. 102, emphasis supplied).

The early church, with its believing Jewish nucleus and believing Gentiles joining in, is described by Paul as the faithful "remnant" of Israel, and as the "Israel of God" (Romans 11:15; Galatians 6:16). In the New Testament, therefore, there is only *one* people of God, and *one* flock and *one* Shepherd in "all dispensations or eras" (ibid., p. 210).

That is why "it is not correct, therefore, to state that the Church has replaced Israel. Rather, the Church is the continuity of the Old

Testament Israel of God; it has only replaced the Jewish nation. Gentile Christians do not constitute a different or separate entity from the faithful remnant of Israel. They are ingrafted into the messianic Israel" (ibid.).

As shown earlier, Jesus didn't ignore the salvation of the Jews, but treated it as a priority. He came to His own first (see John 1:11). He came to save the lost sheep of the house of Israel (see Matthew 15:24). The ones who did not receive Him were not true descendants of Abraham, and by their rejection of the Messiah they cut themselves off from their only Saviour. These are the ones whom Paul refers to as the "Israel after the flesh" (1 Corinthians 10:18).

Jesus is the true Seed of Abraham in whom all the covenant promises are fulfilled. And if we, Jews and Gentiles, are born into Christ the Seed, we become the true offspring of Abraham, "heirs according to the promise" (see Galatians 3:27-29), and "the remnant of her seed which keep the commandments of God, and have the testimony of Jesus Christ" (Revelation, 12:17, KJV). Such faithful remnant of all peoples constitutes the church, which Paul calls the "Israel of God" (Galatians 6:16).

What a loving and wise God we have! He has not changed or wavered in His promises, but in every possible way has tried patiently to save as many of His children as possible. There is no trace of partiality in Him, for He loves everyone, greatly desiring that all come to a saving knowledge of His Son. The apostle Peter, realizing that the gospel of Jesus was freely offered to all, declared: "In truth I perceive that God shows *no partiality*. But in *every* nation whoever fears Him and works righteousness is accepted by Him. The word which God sent to the children of Israel, preaching peace through Jesus Christ—He is Lord of all" (Acts 10:34-36, emphasis supplied).

Accepting Jesus as the Lord of all is what makes anyone, regardless of race, heritage, or background, special to God. "The basis of salvation is not natural descent," writes Walter Specht, "but faith in

Jesus Christ. Salvation is not national, but personal" ("New Testament Israel," *Review and Herald* [November 11, 1976], p. 10). To God's true and universal remnant, Jesus does not become "a stone of stumbling and a rock of offense," but He becomes the "chief cornerstone, elect, precious" (1 Peter 2:6-8).

The vitality of this living chief Cornerstone pervades every stone in His temple. "You also, as living stones, are being built up a spiritual house, a holy priesthood, to offer up spiritual sacrifices acceptable to God through Jesus Christ" (verse 5).

Moreover, through this living Cornerstone, we as the remnant become "a chosen generation, a royal priesthood, a holy nation, His own special people." And God has called such faithful remnant for the same reason He has been calling a remnant throughout history. The apostle Peter gives a resoundingly clear answer: "That you may proclaim the praises of Him who called you out of darkness into His marvelous light" (verse 9).

CHAPTER
8

The Witness of the Remnant
Part One

Y ou are a true son of Abraham," a Muslim religious
leader in West Africa interjected as I was exchanging ideas with him
about what it means to submit ourselves to God. "You would make
a good Muslim," he continued. The word *Muslim* in the Arabic
language refers to a person who submits himself to God. His enthusiastic, complimentary comments were a response to our dialogue as
to what constitutes the character of a true follower of God. In the
course of our animated conversation, I shared with him my personal
testimony of what it means to submit one's life to God as a Christian, interweaving appropriate texts from the Bible and the Koran.

What surprised my Muslim friend was that many Christians in
this world do take their religion seriously. His impression of Christians, reinforced by what he had heard and observed, was that they
were religious in name only. They talked a lot about God's love and

forgiveness, but hardly made an earnest effort in submission and obedience to God, or to follow the example of Jesus in their lives. Thus he concluded that the Christians he had observed were an ungodly lot of people who cared mostly about partying and levity, and carried on a life of immorality and hedonism.

I did my best to assure him that, despite the frivolity he had observed, not all Christians lead such unspiritual lives. I explained that I belonged to a group of Christians who take their God and religion seriously. They are committed Christians who, as a result of God's love and grace, endeavor to live a life of obedience to His commandments and a consecrated life that reflects His character before the world. Astonished and somewhat intrigued by my comments, he wanted to know more about my beliefs and practices as a committed Christian.

Responding to his interest, I proceeded to share with him some of my beliefs and practices. I explained that because our Creator God is the One who made us in His image, we are to glorify Him in maintaining good health: spiritually, mentally, and physically. The human body is a trust given to us by our Creator, and it was intended to be the dwelling place of His Spirit. Therefore, we abstain from defiling and destroying it with alcoholic beverages, tobacco and drugs, unclean foods, and other destructive health practices. God loves us and cares about our health, and He deserves our best efforts in our devotion and service to Him.

The Muslim leader nodded his approval, so I continued to explain that we are against gambling, bingo, and games of chance. We believe in living according to Go ''s Ten Commandments and in maintaining high moral and ethical standards. And in endeavoring, through God's grace, to lead exemplary lives, we shun all immoral and degrading practices, such as drunkenness and promiscuity, trying to avoid even the appearance of evil to prevent being a stumbling block for anyone.

Then we exchanged relevant references from the Bible and the Koran. Today two Koranic verses he quoted still linger in my mind.

"O ye people! Eat of what is on earth, lawful and good. . . . He hath forbidden you dead meat, and blood, and the flesh of swine, and that which any other name hath been invoked besides that of God" (Koran 2:168, 173). Also, "They ask thee concerning wine and gambling. Say: 'In them is great sin, and some profit, for men; but the sin is greater than the profit' " (Koran 2:219).

We moved on to discuss the condition of man in death. According to the Koran, he explained, there is no intervening conscious existence after death. The dead await their resurrection from the grave at the sound of the trumpet, when God comes in judgement upon the world. The dead ones simply rest from their labors as in a sleep, not knowing the passage of time, and only being awakened at the resurrection.

Finally, having discussed several subjects, I introduced him to what the Bible and the Koran have to say about keeping the seventh-day Sabbath holy for the Lord. In seeing corruption among the Jews and Christians and in trying to establish a fresh start and identity, the Muslims rejected keeping holy either the Sabbath of the Jews or the Sunday of the Christians. They chose instead to keep the day before the Sabbath, Friday, as the day for worship.

After listening to the biblical support for Sabbath keeping, the Muslim religious leader was somewhat surprised to discover that God favored the keeping of His Sabbath even in the Koran. I proceeded to read to him from his Arabic Koran the rather strong language concerning the punishment of those who transgress all prohibitions and the Sabbath: "Be ye apes, despised and rejected" (Koran 7:163-166). And then I shared with him the Koranic allusion to the possible reason why Friday was instituted as the day of worship instead of Sabbath. "The Sabbath was only made for those who disagreed; but God will judge between them on the Day of Judgment, as to their differences" (Koran 16:123).

The commentary of Abdullah Yusuf Ali on this verse in his English translation of the Koran is quite revealing. The disputes among Jews and Christians and Christians themselves about the

97

observance of the Sabbath quite likely contributed to the Muslims' ambiguous attitude toward it. "Which was the true Sabbath Day?" Abdullah Ali asks. "The Jews observe Saturday. The Christians, who include the Old Testament in their inspired Scripture, observe Sunday, and a sect among them (the Seventh Day Adventists) disagree, and observe Saturday. So there is disagreement among the people of the Book. Let them dispute among themselves. . . . For them (the Muslims) is the Day of United Prayer on Friday, but it is in no sense like the Jewish or the Scottish Sabbath" (Koran 16:124, p. 689).

This Muslim religious leader kept referring to me as one belonging to "the people of the Book (Bible)." And he was impressed that there are Christians who take the Bible seriously and try to live out its principles. Undoubtedly the Christians' witness to the Muslims has suffered as a result of their disregard of or disagreement with the Word of God. But when Muslims see that there are indeed Christians who, as a result of their faith and loyalty to God, profess and practice all that God reveals in His Word, their attitude can be changed.

Not only can the faithful remnant of Christ effectively witness to the descendants of Abraham through Ishmael, but they can also witness to their cousins, the descendants of Isaac. More than any other Christian denomination, the faithful remnant of Seventh-day Adventists have a unique contribution to make in witnessing to the Jews as well as to the Muslims. The faithful and witnessing remnant is not limited to just the Seventh-day Adventist Christians, but includes faithful ones in all churches.

The witnessing remnant did not start with the advent movement, but functioned from the very beginning of history. Moreover, God has always preserved His remnant to spread His saving knowledge throughout the world. "Adventists repudiate emphatically and unequivocally any thought that they alone are children of God and have a claim upon heaven. They believe that all who worship God in full sincerity, that is, in terms of all the revealed will of God that they understand, are presently potential members of that final 'remnant' company . . . in [Rev.] 12:17" (*SDA Bible Commentary*, vol. 7, p. 815).

What, then, are some of the important characteristics of this faithful remnant of today? They are those who not only built on the truth of the Reformation, but who kept on advancing it. They are the ones whom John the Revelator describes as those "who keep the commandments of God and have the testimony of Jesus Christ" (Revelation 12:17). And they are also referred to by John as: "Here is the patience of the saints; here are those who keep the commandments of God and the faith of Jesus" (Revelation 14:12). "Then the woman fled into the wilderness, where she has a place prepared by God, that they should feed her there one thousand two hundred and sixty days" (Revelation 12:6; see also verse 14; Daniel 7:25).

So the *first* characteristic of this final and faithful remnant is that they have the *faith of Jesus*. This is the kind of faith that trusts completely in the power of God and the truthfulness of His Word.

The *second* characteristic of the last-day remnant is that they *keep the commandments of God*. The living faith of Christ and in Christ is what makes God's remnant people vibrant and victorious in their Christian lives. Their obedience results from their great love of and staunch faith in Christ. They relate to Christ not only as their Saviour, whom they appreciate, but also as the Lord, whom they joyfully obey. They are not only justified by faith in Christ, but they are also sanctified by faith in Christ. For those who say God's commandments are not valid or are not to be obeyed, Jesus Himself clearly says, "If you love Me, *keep My commandments*" (John 14:15, emphasis supplied).

And that clearly means all the Ten Commandments, including the fourth one, which regards keeping holy the seventh-day Sabbath (see Exodus 20:8-11). In this world of idolatry and self-worship, it is no wonder that Satan has been so determined to eradicate this particular commandment that contains the seal of the living God. This commandment reminds people that God is the Creator and that they are to find life and restoration in Him.

The *third* characteristic is that the remnant people of God have *the testimony of Jesus Christ* (see Revelation 12:17). In the Greek this phrase can refer to either the testifying or witnessing that the remnant Christians bear about Christ, or the testimony which has its origin in Jesus and is revealed to humanity through His messenger prophets. However, if we compare this text of Revelation 12:17 with Revelation 19:10, which specifically states that this "testimony of Jesus is the spirit of prophecy," we are led to settle upon the second interpretation. In other words, Jesus testifies concerning Himself through the Holy Spirit's gift of prophecy.

Moreover, studying Revelation 19:10 alongside Revelation 22:9 reinforces this conclusion, for the testimony of Jesus is associated with the ministry of God's prophets. Thus the remnant people in these last days will be distinguished by the manifestation of the gift of prophecy in their midst for the purpose of building up the body of Christ, uplifting Jesus, and helping in accomplishing their mission of preparing a lost world for His second coming. Their Spirit- and truth-filled witness to the world of the gospel of Christ and His soon coming will defeat Satan and give glory to God (see Revelation 12:11). It will encompass a worldwide mission to give triumphantly the gospel commission its final fulfillment (see Matthew 24:14; Revelation 14:6, 7).

The *fourth characteristic* is that this last-day remnant is known for its staunch *faith* in Christ and unflinching *loyalty* to His cause. These are "the ones who follow the lamb wherever He goes" (Revelation 14:4); and they live sanctified lives, for "in their mouth was found no guile, for they are without fault before the throne of God" (verse 5). They follow and obey their Master, not in their own convenient way, but in *all* His ways. They are ready to risk their lives, for "they did not love their lives to the death" (Revelation 12:11) for the sake of Christ.

Finally, they are entrusted with preaching *the three angels' messages* of Revelation 14:6-11. The messages of these angels are fit-

100

tingly tied to the description of the remnant in Revelation 14:4, 5 and Revelation 14:12. The remnant of the advent movement is the only religious body that has been continuously giving these three angels' messages to the world. The most recent and bold evangelistic thrusts throughout the world are a clear indication of this fact. In the last decade and up to the present, this movement has sponsored two worldwide evangelistic campaigns to preach the three angel's messages. The "Thousand Days of Reaping" and "Harvest 90" evangelistic campaigns have resulted in winning thousands of souls to Christ from all corners of the earth. And now it is mobilizing its forces in a bold global strategy to reach the unreached by the end of this century.

Morris Venden sees all the pillars of the advent message embodied in the three angels' messages. These include "the everlasting gospel, the pre-advent judgment, the Sabbath, the law of God, the faith of Jesus, and the condition of mankind in death." Then he explains that "through all of these messages, and through all of the pillars as well, are two threads. The one, warning against self-worship, against trying to save oneself in any way; and the other, an invitation to worship God, to enter into the deeper life of fellowship and communion with Him" (*Uncommon Ground*, p. 19).

As mentioned earlier, more than any other church group, the remnant of the advent movement possess a particular appeal and a unique contribution to reach out to Muslims and Jews. Once I had the occasion to sit next to a Jewish businessman on a flight to Chicago. As we discussed various topics, he was startled to learn that I actually kept the seventh-day Sabbath holy from sundown to sundown, that I cherished the Old Testament, and strongly believed that God's law—the Ten Commandments—is still binding on all Christians. He was also surprised to learn that I followed the instructions in the Old Testament regarding health and avoided unclean foods.

I noticed that he was startled because he had never met Christians before who mentioned such things to him. And that in itself helped to break down barriers so I could freely share other topics from the Scriptures. This revealing experience suggests the likely cause for the interruption of the evangelistic thrust among the Jews after the fourth century A.D. Earlier, the Jews proved quite receptive to Christian evangelism, but as the church started to reject the Sabbath, ignore the law of God, and deemphasize the Torah, the Jews pulled back.

Jacques Doukhan argues that as a result of the church's doctrinal compromises and accommodations, the Jews after the fourth century viewed conversion to Christianity as betrayal of God's law and other important Old Testament teachings. Of course, we know that the first advent of Christ did not destroy the Old Testament, but fulfilled it. Doukhan asserts that "the historical record notes that Christian evangelism, which enjoyed enormous success up to the fourth century among the Jewish masses, suddenly stopped. Israel, in terms of the Law, had been rejected by the Church; and her doors closed to the Jews" (*Drinking at the Sources,* p. 26). He quotes Marcel Simon as saying that "the rejection of Israel by the church beginning with the fourth century, is invariable a corollary to doing away with the Law" (ibid.).

Moreover, in its Council of Laodicea during the fourth century, the church elevated Sunday, the day already revered by the Romans in worshiping the sun, as the holy day for Christians. This accommodation, among others, made it easier yet more superficial for the heathen to become Christians. On the other hand, it made it almost impossible for the Jews to enter. "But to open one door was to close another," argues Doukhan. "By her rejection of the Sabbath, the Church was indeed more successful among the pagans, who could now be incorporated en masse; but by eliminating the major obstacle in the way of the Gentiles, the Church built a major one for the Jews" (ibid., p. 25).

The Jews witnessed with dismay how the Christians were abandoning such doctrines as fundamental as the Sabbath, the law, and other basic biblical doctrines, which neither Jesus nor His apostles in any way disregarded. They witnessed how the Christians were shunning anything that linked them with anything Jewish, no matter how spiritually sound it was. With increasing alarm, the Jews saw that the Christians were abandoning the apostles' and the early church's approach to Jewish evangelism of mainly presenting Jesus as the Messiah. The Christians after the fourth century were not only trying to convert Jews to Christ but also trying to make them abandon anything Jewish, which would obliterate their identity and rich heritage.

As the centuries rolled by, the Jews became even more entrenched in their defensive position of rejecting Christ and Christianity. Their suffering and persecution at the hands of so-called Christians and Christian nations increased; violent anti-Semitism intensified during the Crusades around the eleventh through the thirteenth centuries. Christians' hatred of the Jews grew as Jews were considered traitors and Christ-killers. And all this accumulation of prejudice and hatred against human beings whom God wanted to redeem through His Son culminated in the horrible Holocaust, in which more than six million Jews perished.

The persecutors might have thought that they were exacting vengeance against the Jews in God's behalf. But in their blindness, did they not know that they were crucifying Christ afresh? He desires that *all* should be saved through His infinite and all-sufficient sacrifice. In an article in the *Revue de Paris*, Julian Green asserts that "one cannot strike a Jew without striking with the same blow the Man par excellence, the flower of Israel. It was Jesus they struck in the concentration camps. It is always He, and He never ceases to suffer from it" (cited in Doukhan, p. 39).

But lest we might justify ourselves in condemning other Christians for such abhorrent behavior, we must remember that all of us are capable of such acts, but for the grace of God. Mike Wallace, an investigative reporter of the CBS "60 Minutes" program, narrated a moving story about Yehiel Dinur, a prisoner of a Nazi death camp. When the former prisoner appeared in an Israeli courtroom to confront the Nazi leader Adolf Eichmann, known as the butcher of humanity, he "suddenly began to cry, then fell to the floor. It was not hatred or fear that overcame him. He suddenly realized that Eichmann was not the superman that the inmates had feared; he was an ordinary man."

In reflecting on this unforgettable courtroom experience, Yehiel Dinur said, "I was afraid about myself. I saw that I am capable to do this. I *am . . . exactly like he!*" Mr. Wallace concluded his TV report, concurring with Mr. Dinur and making this strong yet true statement: "Eichmann is in all of us" (Neal C. Wilson, "True Repentance," *Ministry* [July 1990], p. 13).

One can't help but wonder how different the situation might have been had the "Christians" related to and desired the Jews' salvation as much as Jesus and His apostles did prior to the fourth century. We have already seen how Jesus longed to reach out first to the Jews, and how He instructed His disciples before and after His death to go first to the house of Israel.

The apostle Paul's attitude toward the Jews was clearly born out of love, compassion, and an intense desire for them to be saved. Listen to his moving words when he writes: "I have great sorrow and continual grief in my heart. For I could wish that I myself were accursed from Christ for my brethren, my kinsmen according to the flesh" (Romans 9:2, 3). And "brethren, my heart's desire and prayer to God for Israel is that they may be saved" (Romans 10:1).

This same concern for the salvation of his Israelite brethren comes through in the first chapter of his epistle to the Romans: "I am not ashamed of the gospel of Christ, for it is the power of God to salvation for everyone who believes, for the Jew *first* and also for the Greek" (verse 16). Moreover, in addressing the Jews in Acts 13:46, Paul and Barnabas said that before turning to the Gentiles, "it was necessary that the word of God should be spoken to you *first.*" Wherever Paul found himself, his evangelistic strategy was to reach out to the Jews first with the gospel, and then reach out to the Gentiles (see Acts 18:6; 19:8-10).

It is not surprising that God, through His apostle Paul, shows such concern for the Jews' salvation. Even though Israel as a nation had rejected His only Son, He did not reject them as individuals. They remain as precious in His sight as any people from any nation, and He desires to save them as much. Even an earthly father cannot forget his son, no matter how wayward he might be. Though he might even rebel against his father repeatedly and for a long time, the father just cannot forget his very own son. And he hopes that someday he will repent and come home.

Paul explains in Romans how God desires to see the Jews accept His plan of salvation through Christ's righteousness rather than their own, and thereby they would enter the fold of spiritual Israel. Like Paul and many other repentant Jews, the prodigal Jews outside the fold can enter and become a part of spiritual Israel. They may do so like anyone else in the world, if they cease to establish their own righteousness and submit to the righteousness of God (see Romans 10:13).

Quoting the prophet Isaiah, Paul affirms that " 'whoever believes in Him [Christ] will not be put to shame' " (Romans 10:11; see also Isaiah 28:16). That is the only criterion by which anyone can be saved. And Paul goes on to assert that "there is no distinction between Jew and Greek, for the same Lord over all is rich to all who call upon Him" (Romans 10:12). Then, quoting the prophet Joel, he continues, "Whoever calls upon the name of the Lord shall be saved" (Romans 10:13; see also Joel 2:32). "God has provided only one means whereby men may be saved. He does not have one provision for the Jew and another for the Gentile. Hence all national, class, social, and individual distinctions vanish" (*SDA Bible Commentary,* vol. 6, p. 599).

Some Christian groups advocate what is called the "two-covenant theory," that the Jews are saved, or will be saved on a different basis than the rest of humankind. This theory goes against the teachings of the New Testament as well the Old Testament. Simply stated, this particular theory teaches that the "Jews, because of God's unique relationship with them since Abraham, need not believe in Christ for salvation" (Pamela Pearson Wong, "Document Angers Jewish Community," *Christianity Today* [September 22, 1989], p. 48).

Paul served as great proof that God is quite willing and ready to accept any Christ-believing Jew: "I say then, has God cast away His people? Certainly not! For I also am an Israelite, of the seed of Abraham, of the tribe of Benjamin" (Romans 11:1). Then he continues to show that God's special treatment of the Jews as a nation had caused them to take Him for granted and finally reject His Son, their only Hope.

God longs to have everyone accept His Son Jesus for salvation, so why wouldn't He be as willing to gladly save a Jew through acceptance of Christ? Such salvation of a Jew can be considered significant, for the Lord has dealt with the children of Israel for many centuries, revealing Himself through their prophets and finally culminating with the incarnation of His only divine Son as one of them.

He dealt with them like no other people, and for many centuries they had the benefit of His nurture and discipline. These facts of history cannot be erased or simply forgotten. Paul depicts them as the ones "to whom pertain the adoption, the glory, the covenants, the giving of the law, the service of God, and the promises; of whom are the fathers and from whom, according to the flesh, Christ came, who is over all, the eternally blessed God" (Romans 9:4, 5).

We must remember that Jesus, Paul, and the other apostles, who were all Jews, did not abandon their Jewishness as such. They did not suddenly discard their rich heritage and history, the prophets, the law, and the promises and prophecies. True biblical Judaism does not carelessly throw out all of that, but rather builds on it and finds its meaning and fulfillment in the Messiah.

In reaching out to the Jews, our priority should not be simply to overthrow their religion. In the spirit of acceptance, tact, and love, we need to help them see their religion in the light of the gospel of Christ. Like Paul, we are to proclaim to the Jews, not "a Messiah whose work is to destroy the old dispensation, but a Messiah who came to develop the whole Jewish economy in accordance with the truth" (*Evangelism*, p. 554). "The most convincing proof was given [by Paul] that the gospel was but the *development* of the Hebrew faith" (*Sketches From the Life of Paul*, p. 104, emphasis supplied).

The reason why God chose ancient Israel remains the same as His reason for choosing spiritual Israel. He chose the children of Israel and made them special, not for their own sake, but rather for the glorious purpose of blessing the other nations with His saving knowledge. Likewise, God founded the Christian church so that again, the saving knowledge of the gospel might reach the entire world. In the great gospel commission, Jesus commanded His disciples to "go therefore and make disciples of all the nations, baptizing them in the name of the Father and of the Son and of the Holy Spirit" (Matthew 28:19).

The Jews are certainly to be included in the wide scope of this gospel commission to the church. And to overlook the Jews or any other group in evangelism is to betray its very existence. As a consequence of the church's neglect to reach out to the Jews after the fourth century, it's likely that they became more spiritually isolated and hardened against the gospel of Christ. Hence, the church bears great responsibility for that.

Such neglect has also contributed to the church's disregard for the immutable law of God. "Jesus, looking down to the last generation, saw the world involved in a deception similar to that which caused the destruction of Jerusalem. The great sin of the Jews was their rejection of Christ; the great sin of the Christian world would be their rejection of the law of God, the foundation of His government in heaven and earth" (*The Great Controversy*, p. 22). Other major doctrines disregarded were the enduring validity of the seventh-day Sabbath; the relevance of the sanctuary doctrine in connection with the high-priestly ministry of Christ in the heavenly sanctuary; the continuing authoritativeness of the Old Testament; and the emphasis on honoring God in our health, diet, and lifestyle.

We can say with certainty that if the church had continued its Christian dialogue and witness to the Jews, it would not have easily discarded the biblical doctrines listed above. For such Christian-Jewish interaction would have kept these subjects alive.

God has restored His precious truths, discarded and trodden underfoot, through His faithful remnant. In these crucial last days of earth's history, He wants His witnessing remnant to reach out to the Jews and win their trust by presenting them with these restored truths. This is precisely the *unique* advantage that Seventh-day Adventists have, and the *unique* contribution we can make in effectively witnessing to the Jews. The advent message has a built-in advantage that other denominations simply do not possess.

We who are greatly privileged to be the witnesses who "keep the commandments of God and the faith of Jesus" (Revelation 14:12) and who preach the three angels' messages of Revelation 14 must rise to the task of evangelizing the present descendants of Abraham more than ever before. This is our unique evangelistic opportunity. Shall we not take advantage of it as did the apostles and the early church? God forbid that we recklessly squander it as the apostate church had done!

CHAPTER
9

The Witness of the Remnant
Part Two

Would the real Jew please stand up? Who is the real Jew these days anyway? In the modern state of Israel, a Jew can believe in practically anything or believe in nothing, and still be regarded a Jew. A Jew who is an atheist, agnostic, secularist, humanist, New Ager, or whatever, can legally be considered a Jew; yet a Jew who believes in Jesus as the Messiah cannot. On December 25, 1989, the supreme court of the state of Israel handed down the decision that Jews who believe in Christ are not readily or automatically granted Israeli citizenship (see *Christianity Today* [February 5, 1990], p. 57).

This question of "who is a Jew" was on the minds of the Israeli leaders and Jewish scholars in 1948, when the state of Israel was established. Therefore, two years later, in 1950, the Parliament of Israel created the "Law of Return," allowing returning Jews from around the world automatic Israeli citizenship. This law stipulated that a Jew is a person born to a Jewish mother or one who converts to Judaism, adhering to no other religions (see Lyn Cryderman, "Who Is a Jew?" *Christianity Today* [February 19, 1990], p. 10).

So a Jew born of a Jewish mother who accepts Jesus as the promised Messiah cannot readily become a citizen of Israel. He has to go through the routine channels reserved to the Gentile applicants. This transpired when a South African couple, who call themselves Messianic Jews, requested citizenship. The Israeli supreme court deliberated this delicate case and handed down a landmark decision at the end of 1989. Menachem Elon, one of the justices of the Israeli supreme court, wrote, "Those who believe in Jesus are, in fact, Christians" (ibid.).

Rabbi Morris Kertzer finds the whole question of who is a Jew a puzzling one. He wonders whether being a Jew is a matter of condition or conviction. Then he goes on to suggest three definitions: one, a *religious* definition; two, a *cultural* definition; and three, a *practical* definition (see Rosten, pp. 142, 143). Most of the Jews, however, consider themselves Jewish because of cultural and practical reasons. It is often a matter of racial, cultural, and nationalistic identity, and pride in the rich heritage and history of the Jewish people.

What constitutes a Jew is by no means a new argument. The Jews of Christ's day debated with Him to prove that they were the true Jews and true children of Abraham. And Jesus responded to their prideful claim by defining for them what really determines who a true son of Abraham is: "If you were Abraham's children, you would *do the works of Abraham*" (John 8:39, emphasis supplied). The name *Israel* means "God-ruled," referring to those who submit themselves to God and allow Him to rule in their lives.

The apostle Paul affirms this concept when he explains that the true Israelites are those who are the children of promise. They are those who believe in God's promises and trust in what God can do to save them, through the sacrifice of the Lamb whom He provided.

He writes that "they are not all Israel who are of Israel, nor are they all children because they are the seed of Abraham" (Romans 9:6, 7; see also verses 8-11). Happily, however, among the Jews there have always been children of the promise who believe like Abraham and do his works.

In His faithfulness to His people, God has not forgotten those who have been earnestly seeking Him. For "there have lived from age to age many noble, God-fearing Jewish men and women who have suffered in silence. God has comforted their hearts in affliction and has beheld with pity their terrible situation. He has heard the agonizing prayers of those who have sought Him with all the heart for the right understanding of His world. Some have learned to see in the lowly Nazarene whom their forefathers rejected and crucified, the true Messiah of Israel. . . . It is to this class that Isaiah referred in prophecy, 'A remnant shall be saved' " (Rosten, pp. 379, 380). Indeed even prior to Christ's first advent, a remnant spiritual Israel had always existed in the midst of a larger literal Israel (see Romans 9:27; 11:1-4).

In the unified theme of Romans 9 to 11, the apostle Paul seems to indicate that some of the Jews who were cut off from the olive tree because of unbelief will be grafted into spiritual Israel on the condition that they believe in the gospel of Jesus. Such spiritual restoration will not take place automatically, merely because they belong to the literal stock of Abraham, but because they will repent and accept Christ as Saviour and Lord. Paul doesn't say that the salvation of such Christ-believing Jews is to be understood in a literal ethnic or racial sense. And it is not to be based on any human righteousness but on having faith in Christ and His righteousness.

Such conditions for becoming a part of the remnant of spiritual Israel apply to all individuals, regardless of who they are or when they live. The same conditions for salvation are valid in the New Testament as well as the Old. For God is no respecter of persons, He is unchangeable, and it is against His nature to coerce the will of anyone to accept Him. He does all He can to draw all to Him, but they need to freely and wholeheartedly decide to join themselves to Him. " 'Whoever calls upon the name of the Lord shall be saved' " (Romans 10:13; see also verses 9-12).

Hans LaRondelle, in his recent presentation "One Saviour—One People" before a group of Adventist theologians in Indianapolis (July 1990), stated that "Christian faith is not in conflict with the faith of ancient Israel. The Christian way of salvation and sanctification is rather the advancement and unfolding of the Hebrew faith. Christian faith is only in conflict with a legalistic or self-righteous Judaism, because that represents a deviation from the faith of the patriarchs. Christian faith accepts the whole OT as God's covenant of grace" (pp. 7, 8).

The restoration which Paul addresses is *spiritual restoration*. That applies not only to the Jews, but to all people. The Jewish leaders stubbornly wanted Jesus to establish a *physical* kingdom, but He stressed the fact over and over again that His kingdom was to be a *spiritual* one. With the ending of the seventy-week prophetic period (490 literal years, beginning in 457 B.C. and ending in A.D. 34) allotted to the Jewish nation, or political entity (see Daniel 9:24-27), God's plan was not to choose another temporal power or another theocracy to accomplish His purposes in the world. He had another plan.

His divine plan was to choose a spiritual entity, the Christian church or spiritual Israel, to witness to the world. That is what He meant when He told the Jewish leaders that "the kingdom of God will be taken from you and given to a nation bearing the fruits of it" (Matthew 21:43). God's greatest interest and desire has been to establish a genuine, witnessing remnant brought together from all peoples for the crucial purpose of preparing the world for His Son's second coming.

The apostle Paul's specific theme in Romans 9 to 11 is the spiritual restoration of a faithful universal remnant of God. His emphasis is spiritual and universal rather than temporal and nationalistic. His focus is on the gathering of a spiritual remnant, centered in Christ, coming from all the world and reaching out to all the world.

In studying these chapters in Romans, one senses that Paul envisions a time at the end when the Jews will choose to have a greater response to the gospel of Christ than before. After all, that was his great burden: to win the Jews to the gospel. "If by any means I may provoke to jealousy those who are my flesh [the Jews] and save some of them" (Romans 11:14).

Paul talks about a "mystery" that he does not want us to be ignorant of, that a "hardening in part has happened to Israel until the fullness of the Gentiles has come in" (Romans 11:25). Such a willing acceptance of Christ on the part of present-day Jews can come about through the active witness of His church. As a result of the long history of special dealings with them, it is understandable that God, just before the second coming of Christ, might endeavor to give them a special and final appeal to accept the gospel of His Son.

Through this special appeal the responsive Jews will be grafted in the olive tree, and thus will join the last remnant ready to meet Christ in His glory. And although the majority of them continue to reject the gospel, it does not mean that the principle of God's election to salvation has ceased for them if they believe.

Even though the Jews are in the state of being enemies of the gospel, God still loves them and longs to see them saved. Paul again writes of them: "Concerning the gospel they are enemies for your sake, but concerning the election they are beloved for the sake of the fathers" (Romans 11:28). He cannot forget them as people, as precious individuals for whom Christ shed His blood. How could God forget them, and how could He not love them and want them to join the saved universal remnant! He movingly declares through Isaiah: "Can a woman forget her nursing child, and not have compassion on the son of her womb? Surely they may forget, yet I will not forget you. See, I have inscribed you on the palms of My hands" (Isaiah 49:15, 16).

He cannot forget the special relationship He had with their fathers Abraham, Isaac, and Jacob, and all the other patriarchs and prophets. God is like a father who invests many precious years of his life in a wayward child. He simply cannot help remembering his son and, in his great love, desiring him to come back and be restored. Of course he can choose not to, but that does not change how a father feels. God describes Himself as a Father. He says, "I am a Father to Israel, and Ephraim is My firstborn" (Jeremiah 31:9).

Paul moves on to introduce the idea of the "fullness" of the Jews (see Romans 11:12) and the "fullness of the Gentiles" (verse 25). What does this "fullness" signify? How does this relate to the "hardening in part" on the part of the Jews referred to in Romans 11:25? Paul seems to indicate that somehow the unbelieving Jews will have a softening of heart so that they may appreciate the gift of salvation through Christ. How does the "fullness" of the Gentiles relate to the "fullness" of the Jews? Will God, through the effective witness of His remnant church, give a mighty appeal to the unbelieving Jews in these last days just prior to Christ's second coming?

Paul's major concern is evangelism to the Jews. He is very concerned about their salvation and is earnestly seeking to save at least some. The "hardening in part" implies that not all Jews were hardened, but that some accepted the Messiah, forming the nucleus of spiritual Israel. God mightily used this witnessing remnant, made up of the apostles and other Christ-believing Jews, to preach the gospel to the Gentiles. In his anxiousness to see at least some Jews accept the gospel, the apostle Paul seems clearly to be appealing to the believing Gentiles to be evangelistically reciprocal to the Jews. Such may make them envious of their salvation, so the Jews too might desire it for themselves (see Romans 11:11, 14).

This realistic and evangelistic argument of Paul's makes sense. For when the Jews witness the great salvation enjoyed by the Gentiles and the great spiritual transformation it has wrought in their lives, they may envy what they are missing. After all, these spiritual blessings were initially intended for them. How can they let the believing Gentiles enjoy them all to themselves? Such a positive reaction on the part of his "kinsmen according to the flesh" would certainly make Paul very happy indeed.

LaRondelle stresses this reciprocity, which he describes as returning the favor. "The tidal wave of the gospel," he says, "went from Israel to the Gentiles *in order that* this wave may return from the Gentiles to the Jews. That is the challenging apocalyptic mystery that Paul develops in Romans 11" ("One Saviour—One People," pp. 9, 10).

Here is the Pauline text at the heart of our discussion: "I do not desire, brethren, that you should be ignorant of this mystery, lest you should be wise in your own opinion, that hardening in part has happened to Israel until the fullness of the Gentiles has come in. And so all Israel will be saved" (Romans 11:25, 26). The term *fullness* of the Gentiles found in this interesting text is a translation of the Greek word *pleroma*. And in the RSV it is rendered as the "full number" of the Gentiles.

Does this mean that the apostle Paul believes that God will eventually save all the Gentiles, regardless of their response to the gospel? By no means, for this would go contrary to what he himself consistently taught about salvation. In the Pauline theology of salvation, a person must respond to God's initiative, as is clearly seen in Romans 10:9-13. There we see Paul employing conditional language in relation to accepting Christ: "If you confess," "if . . . you believe," "whoever believes," and "whoever calls." In other words, Paul is referring to the "full number," or all of the Gentiles who meet the indispensable prerequisite of confessing and believing in Christ. These Christ-believing Gentiles are the ones fitted to "come in" to the fold of spiritual Israel.

This allusion to the "fullness of the Gentiles" coming in (Romans 11:25) is immediately followed by the reference to "all Israel will be saved" in verse 26. The expression "all Israel" is closely connected to the expression "the full number of the Gentiles." In fact, the *same* Greek word *pleroma*, used in reference to the Gentiles, is *also* used in reference to the Jews in Romans 11:12. "If their [the Jews'] fall is riches for the world, and their failure riches for the Gentiles, how much more *their fullness*" (emphasis supplied). "Their fullness," of course, refers to the *fullness of the Jews.*

This interdependence between the references to the fullness of the Gentiles and the fullness of the Jews becomes even more certain when we understand the meaning of the two small Greek words, *kai houtos,* at the very beginning of Romans 11:26. The conjunction *kai,* translated as "and," may also be rendered "in addition to," "as well as," or "as a consequence," in direct reference to what was just mentioned in the preceding verse. And *houtos,* translated as "so," may also be rendered "in this way," "thus," "in the same way," and "like this" (Bruce M. Metzger, ed., *The Greek New Testament Dictionary,* 2nd edition, p. 129).

The *SDA Bible Commentary* states that the "adverb [*so*] expresses manner, not conclusion, or time" (vol. 6, p. 611). Therefore, in addition to the "fullness of the Gentiles" coming in, in the same way, "all Israel will be saved." In other words, the Jews will be saved in the same manner as the Gentiles are being saved. And this is the *only* way of salvation for all people and at all times: through believing in Christ. "For there is *no distinction* between Jew and Greek, for the same Lord over all is rich to *all* who call upon Him" (Romans 10:12, emphasis supplied).

So as a consequence of the gathering-in of all the Christ-believing Gentiles in the last days, under the great power of the latter rain, the Jews will be incited to be saved too. Does this mean literally *all* of the Jews, regardless of their response to the gospel? Paul writes, "And so all Israel will be saved" (Romans 11:26). Does he mean literally all of the Jews living at the time of the end will be saved, regardless of their acceptance or rejection of Christ? By no means.

According to some interpreters, the statement, "all Israel will be saved," may refer to all believing Jews and Gentiles. But from the context, it likely refers to all the Jews who will freely choose to accept Christ. Many will make this decision as a result of being envious of a tremendous conversion among the Gentiles, and also as a result of being witnessed to by those believing Gentiles. Thus the partial hardening of the Jews, or the hardening of heart of some of them against the gospel, will again be softened by the powerful witness of the gospel.

Paul writes about the "hardening in part" that has happened to Israel, referring to the unbelieving Jews who were represented by the olive branches lopped off the olive tree. These are the ones who will be given the opportunity to accept the salvation offered by Christ (if they so freely choose), and be grafted back into the olive tree.

However, Paul cautions that remaining connected to the tree is as crucial as the initial connection or grafting. He does not teach here universalism or "once saved, always saved" theology, but rather the indispensable conditions one must fulfill to remain connected to the olive tree. Conditionalism is evident when he thus admonishes the believing Gentiles in Romans 11:22, 23: "Consider the goodness and severity of God: on those who fell, severity; but toward you, goodness, *if you continue* in His goodness. Otherwise you also will be cut off." Then he turns with hope to the unbelieving Jews, explaining that *"if* they do not continue in unbelief, [they] will be grafted in, for God is able to graft them in" (emphasis supplied).

Hans LaRondelle affirms that "the condition for the salvation of all Israel is crystal clear: they must not persist in their unbelief regarding Messiah Jesus and in their opposing the gospel proclamation (see 1 Thessalonians 2:14-16)." Then looking at the last days, just before the second return of Jesus, he stresses that the "Jews cannot be saved at the second advent if they have persistently rejected the atoning death of Christ. God does not have a different gospel or a way of salvation in the future for those who have willfully rejected Christ's first advent. The Jew must kneel at the foot of the cross, just like every Gentile prior to the judgment day" ("One

Saviour—One People," p. 14).

In Romans 11:26, Paul appeals to David and Isaiah in combining two of their Messianic prophecies relating to Christ's first advent (see Psalm 14:7; Isaiah 59:21). He writes, " 'The Deliverer will come out of Zion, and He will turn away ungodliness from Jacob; for this is My covenant with them, when I take away their sins.' "

God was not slack in sending the promised Messiah. He sent His only Son to be incarnated as a Jew in Israel, dwelling among the Jewish people. Despite their resistance to Him, He patiently ministered to them and ultimately gave His life for their salvation and the salvation of the world. So all provisions were made for their salvation. Heaven could do no more than give the Son of God. The crucial question is not about God's love and willingness to save, but about the kind of response the Jews give to His offer of salvation now and in the near future.

Will they accept the Messiah's first coming? Will they accept it now? What are we doing to help bring this about? Does our Christian example and our Christlike character incite them to respond to the gospel? Will they accept His second coming in the clouds of glory? Without the acceptance of Christ's first coming as the Sacrifice and Saviour, they will not accept Him when He comes as the King of kings. But "how then shall they call on Him in whom they have not believed? And how shall they believe in Him of whom they have not heard? And how shall they hear without a preacher? And how shall they preach unless they are sent?" (Romans 10:14, 15).

This must be the battle cry of evangelism for the remnant in these last days. As we appeal to the unreached people groupings around the globe during this decade, we must not overlook the unreached Jews. Neither can we ignore the more than eight hundred million unreached Muslims in the world. Reaching the unreached is the advent movement's global evangelistic strategy for the end of this century. That was the important and awesome challenge given at the General Conference session in Indianapolis in July of

1990 (see the *Adventist Review,* July 5 and 12, 1990).

But that is humanly impossible without the work of the Holy Spirit in Pentecostal proportions. For "He will finish the work and cut it short in righteousness" (Romans 9:28). If He could use a few disciples who were filled and empowered with the Holy Spirit to turn the world upside down, why can't He use millions of us to finish the task of spreading the gospel to the entire world?

Ellen White makes a glorious prediction of what will happen in the last days when the Pentecostal experience will be repeated among the ranks of God's faithful remnant. "Servants of God, with their faces lighted up and shining with holy consecration, will hasten from place to place to proclaim the message from heaven. By thousands of voices, all over the earth, the warning will be given. Miracles will be wrought, the sick will be healed, and signs and wonders will follow the believers. . . . Thus the inhabitants of the earth will be brought to take their stand" (*The Great Controversy,* p. 612). Moreover, she affirms that "the message will be carried not so much by argument as by the deep conviction of the Spirit of God" (ibid.).

Ellen White ascertains that our commission to work for the salvation of the Jews is found in the eleventh chapter of Romans. Pentecostal power will be given to the witnessing remnant to accomplish this challenging task.

"The time has come when the Jews are to be given light. The Lord wants us to encourage and sustain men who shall labor in right lines for this people; for there are to be a multitude convinced of the truth, who will take their position for God." Then she prophetically adds that "the time is coming when there will be *as many* converted in a day as there were on the day of Pentecost, after the disciples had received the Holy Spirit" ("The Need of Home Religion," *Review and Herald* [June 29, 1905], emphasis supplied). It is recorded in Acts 2:41 that on that particular day when Peter preached Christ to the Jews, about three thousand souls gladly received Christ and were baptized and added to the early church.

The Lord has graciously given us numerous and very pertinent counsels through Ellen White regarding the urgent work with the Jews. Not many can be included here, but suffice it to mention a few. We learn that "in the *closing proclamation* of the gospel, when special work is to be done for *classes of people hitherto neglected*, God expects His messengers to take *particular interest in the Jewish people* whom they find in all parts of the earth" (*The Acts of the Apostles,* p. 381, emphasis supplied). This is the very period in our history when our church leaders are mobilizing God's people to reach those "classes of people hitherto neglected" around the world. The Jewish people, the Muslims, and other unreached people must be reached prior to Christ's coming.

What are the right qualifications and the most effective methods to use in meeting this challenge? The first qualification is to be a converted Christian, presenting the fruits of the Spirit in a transformed life, a life that reveals the love and life of Christ. Such a life, fired up by the anointing of the Holy Spirit, is a powerhouse in this world. A transformed and sanctified life, combined with Christ's and the New Testament's methods, will yield a great harvest for the kingdom. In thoroughly contemplating the life of Christ in the four Gospels, Ellen White gleaned from their pages Christ's effective method in reaching people.

The great need of the world is for Christ to be revealed in His people's lives. How is that to be done? One powerful way is through following Christ's example of witnessing. For His "method alone will give true success in reaching the people" (*The Ministry of Healing,* p. 143). Then she briefly mentions five points contained in this method. "The Saviour *mingled* with men as one who desired their good. He showed His *sympathy* for them, ministered to their *needs,* and won their *confidence.* Then He bade them, 'Follow Me' " (emphasis supplied).

The author has taken this paragraph and developed it into a book entitled simply *Christ's Way of Reaching People,* in which he carefully discusses all these steps. You may refer to it, if you so wish, for further study on this important subject. You too may experience Christ's method in your life; for this method, "accompanied by the power of persuasion, the power of prayer, the power of the love of God . . . will not, cannot, be without fruit" (ibid., pp. 143, 144).

A booklet entitled *What Ellen G. White Says About Work for the Jewish People*, published in 1976, presents some helpful ideas for witnessing to the Jews. Here they are in brief: First, blend the Old Testament with the New Testament and show how well they relate to each other. Second, use the keys of the Old Testament to unlock the doors of the New Testament.

Third, study Paul's approach to the Jews. In order not to arouse their prejudice, he first discussed the subjects that interested them, such as the law and the prophecies, which gradually led to the subject of the promised Messiah. Fourth, present the sanctuary services and show how the services of the earthly sanctuary relate to the services of the heavenly sanctuary. Fifth, discuss the prophecies relating to the promised Messiah. Sixth, prove from the Scriptures the identity of the Messiah, showing that all the religious services and ceremonies have no real meaning without the Messiah (pp. 6-9).

In addition, here are some helpful suggestions in reaching out to Muslims: First, nurture a genuine relationship, for Muslims respond greatly to friendship, love, and hospitality. Remember that they are people oriented. Second, discuss the religious common ground you have with them. Listen, sympathize, understand, and win their trust.

Third, introduce them to the Bible, so they may learn the true identity of Christ. The best books to start with are the Gospels of John and Matthew. John, because it begins with describing Jesus as "the Word of God," a title of Christ with which they are already familiar, as mentioned earlier in this book. Matthew, because it traces the genealogy of Jesus back to David and Abraham, and mentions Jesus' birth from a virgin. And as we have discovered earlier in this book, these subjects are acceptable to them.

Fourth, witness from your relationship with God. Describe the inner peace and the assurance of salvation you experience as a result of submitting yourself completely to Him. Often they are not sure of their own salvation and whether their works are ever good enough. They are in desperate need of a Saviour.

Fifth, don't spend your time arguing. You may win a few battles in the process, but you will likely lose the war for their hearts. Finally, let them clearly see the living and loving Christ manifest Himself through you. Most Muslims who were converted to Christ were converted as a result of the genuine Christian love of a faithful friend. The Holy Spirit will bless your authentic example, and, as a result, touch their hearts, convicting them of the truth in ways they did not expect (see Seamands, pp. 213, 214).

Furthermore, when Jews or Muslims accept the gospel of Christ and join your church fellowship, continue to show genuine concern, acceptance, love, and friendship. I have witnessed Jews and Muslims who accepted the gospel eventually leave the Christian fellowship for not having been accepted and loved by the church members. Individuals who become Christians from these two religious groups take a tremendous risk of becoming ostracized by their own people. It is imperative that they find a haven of acceptance and friendship in the Christian community.

No matter how refined or ethical, believers of both Judaism and Islam desperately need a Saviour and the assurance of salvation. Both religions, for their own reasons, reject Christ as the Messiah and Saviour of the world. These children of Abraham desperately need Christ, the Promised Seed. Without Him, their religions are incapable of satisfying the deepest longings and fulfilling the greatest desires of the human soul. We know for certain that they and all humankind need Christ the Saviour. But how do we effectively lead them to Him? The answer is not found in amassing more proofs or arguments, but ultimately in reaching the human heart and soul through the promised miraculous power of the Holy Spirit.

Love for souls, energized and guided by Pentecostal power, will give Christians wisdom—such as Paul had—in knowing how to witness effectively.

"I have freely and happily become a servant of any and all so that I can win them to Christ. When I am with the Jews, I seem as one of them so that they will listen to the Gospel and I can win them to Christ. When I am with the Gentiles who follow Jewish customs and ceremonies I don't argue, even though I don't agree, because I want to help them. . . . Yes, whatever a person is like, I try to find common ground with him so that he will let me tell him about Christ and let Christ save him" (1 Corinthians 9:19-22, Taylor's Translation).

An unforgettable account that I heard some years ago forcefully conveys how the Holy Spirit can work miraculously on the human heart of any religious background. One devout Muslim was studying about Christ, but was unsure and not yet able to accept Him as the Saviour of the world. One night in his sleep he had a dream. From a distance he saw several tombs of various religious founders. Curiously approaching them, he noticed that only one of the tombs was empty. Anxious to know to whom this empty grave belonged, he noticed its headstone with the inscription and the ultimate answer to his perplexing dilemma: "Jesus Christ the living Son of God, and Saviour of the world." Praise God, we serve a *risen Saviour!*

CHAPTER

10

The Land Promised

I swear to God," Iraqi president Saddam Hussein began his ominous threat heard around the world, "we will let our fire scorch half of Israel if it tries to wage anything against us" ("The World's Most Dangerous Man," *U.S. News & World Report* [June 4, 1990], p. 39). The war-hardened Hussein, who styles himself as the "Sword of the Arabs," invoked this oath in response to possible Israeli threats to launch preemptive strikes against Iraq's miltary, nuclear, and chemical facilities. And Israel was willing to prove that when, in 1981, its bombers launched a sudden attack, destroying the Iraqis' nuclear reactor at Osirak. It wouldn't be suprising at all if Israel repeats such military action in the future. While peace and democracy seem to be springing up throughout the world, more than ever the Middle East seems to be drawing the world into war.

And although the Gulf War had been fought and won against

Iraq, attacks, threats and counter threats continue. What makes the situation so volatile is the unreconcilable differences and hardened positions of the antagonists.

All this is fueled by the globally strategic importance of the Middle East–economically, geographically, politically and religiously. Moreover, the embitterment and despair of the Palestinians over the lack of progress in culminating a comprehensive and lasting peace agreement between them and the Israelis. Both sides are adamant about what they claim to be their sacred rights to the land of their ancestors.

The Palestinians' use of stones in their uprising escalates into other more serious acts of violence, only to be met by swift Israeli retaliation. Grief and death becomes a way of life; and how can that stop while both sides tenaciously hold on to the same land of their father Abraham. These feuding relatives are forced to agree that violence and death has got to stop, but *how* can that be accomplished is the big question.

And try as they may, real peace seems evermore like an elusive dream to them. The Israelis recognize that their Palestinian neighbors are there to stay, that their plight cannot anymore be ignored or their voices silenced. On the other hand, it is finally dawning on the Palestinians and their Arab allies that Israel, with its military superiority and support from the United States, cannot be pushed into the sea.

The sudden collapse of Communism in the former Soviet Union and Eastern Europe leaves the United States the sole super power in the world. Consequently the Palestinians are forced to look to this super power to be more engaged as an even-handed broker for peace, and to help put pressure on Israel. They are encouraged when they sometimes hear that the American leadership considers the continuing Israeli settlements as an obstacle to peace. Yet the Jewish state goes on building new settlements in what they consider an integral part of the land of Israel.

God's ideal for this special land in the Middle East was to reveal His character of peace and holiness to the entire world. Strategically located between the continents of Asia, Africa and Europe, God desired to make an impact on all of humanity. Regrettably, this has not often been the case. On the contrary, Jerusalem (*Yerushalayim* in Hebrew, *Urashalim* in Arabic), "the city of peace" has not known much but violence, and the Holy Land has not shown much but the unholy. What poor representations of the New Jerusalem and the New Earth!

The vicious and relentless cycle of violence in this *long-running* family feud of blood brothers goes unabated. Revenge, tit-for-tat has become the order of the day. The Palestinians feel they have nothing to lose in lashing out against those who occupy their land. And you can always count on Israel to exact swift and disproportionate retaliation. Thus revengeful attack followed by counter attack becomes a way of life while both sides suffer misery and death.

It is not so secret that Israel has possessed nuclear weapons for some years, and that other countries of this turbulent region are trying to acquire the same capabilities of weapons of mass destruction. Iraq has missiles that can deliver poison gas to many capitals of neighboring countries. Who knows what another round of fighting in the Middle East will bring about. Will that be the ushering in of a showdown at Armageddon?

What a troubled land! Not many people remember that region experiencing anything but turmoil. What is it about that paticular region of the world to generate this kind of perpetual conflict? Someone once said in jest that the problem with the Promised Land is that it was promised to too many peoples. Nowhere in the world is there a piece of real estate so coveted and fought for as the Holy Land. Over countless generations, the land has been occupied in turn by the Palestinians, the Hebrews, the Assyrians, the Persians, the Greeks, the Romans, the Muslims, the Crusaders, the Muslims again, the Egyptians, the Turks, the British, and now the Jews.

Why are so many people interested in Israel, and why is that part of the Middle East constantly in the news media? When American astronaut Neil Armstrong visited Jerusalem after becoming the first man to step on the moon, he was taken on a tour by Israeli archae-ologist Meir Ben-Dov. When they got to the stairs leading to the

Temple Mount, Armstrong asked Ben-Dov whether Jesus did actually walk anywhere there. The following dialogue ensued between this Christian and Jew about Jesus:

"I told him 'Look, Jesus was a Jew,' " recalled Ben-Dov. "These are the steps that lead to the Temple, so he must have walked here many times." Armstrong kept on pressing his guide to confirm to him if those steps they were walking on were actually the very steps that Jesus walked on.

"So Jesus stepped right here?" asked Armstrong again.

"That's right," answered Ben-Dov.

"I have to tell you," Armstrong said to the Israeli archaeologist, "I am more excited stepping on these stones than I was stepping on the moon" (Friedman, *From Beirut to Jerusalem*, p. 429).

It is true that the Holy Land is unique in that sense. The very Son of God, the Creator of the universe, actually walked on the soil of that part of the world. And if we were living there during that time of history, we would have possibly greeted Him, realizing that we shook hands and talked to our very Creator!

Thomas Friedman, because of the Western world's focus on the Holy Land, calls the Bible the "super story." And "when looked at this way, Israel becomes one of the largest of countries in the eyes of the West" (ibid., p. 428). This super story makes the events very important, such as the event of God giving the Ten Commandments to Moses on Mount Sinai. The impact of these commandments proved to be of epic proportion, for they served as the very foundation of what we call the Judeo-Christian standards of ethics and morality.

Unfortunately, today, regardless of all that God did in their behalf, the Jewish leaders, as well as the Jewish people in Israel, still persist in unbelief. God made them the apple of His eye, blessing them more than any other nation, and finally even giving His own Son to save them. Yet, till this day, they still resist Christian evangelism and continue to cling to their legalistic religion and nationalistic ambitions, devoid of their only Saviour, Jesus Christ.

In fact, it is difficult for a Jew to accept Christ and become a Christian. The same thing applies to a Muslim. Christians may choose to change their religion with relative ease and without much opposition from their families and friends. Yet when it comes to a Jew or a Muslim exercising the same right, it is often a tortuous ordeal. Listen to what Jacob Gartenhaus writes in describing the converted Jew's experience: "The Jew, on becoming a Christian, might immediately and cruelly be ostracized from his people; his parents would lament him as dead and curse his memory, and his friends would turn to be his implacable adversaries" (*Unto His Own,* p. 35).

But Christians are not blameless for this terrible resistance to the gospel of Christ. For many centuries they have presented a distorted gospel and misrepresented Christ in their lives. They have used their Christian religion to persecute the Jews. In a sense, the Jews were forced to take an extreme defensive position because they saw in the conversion to Christianity a denial of their identity as a people and a betrayal of their biblical heritage.

They simply could not abandon all that had held them together against a persecuting Christian world and surrender to their implacable enemies. That would be treason, a betrayal to those who would say "join us or else!" Conversion meant the total abolishment of everything Jewish, regardless of how spiritually valid or unchangeable it was.

As mentioned in an earlier chapter, what made it so difficult for the Jews to consider Christianity was its pernicious distortion and corruption. The loving Christ was eclipsed from the view of the Jews, and instead a vengeful Christ was poised to exact retribution. In this connection, Nicolai Berdyaev appropriately commented that "Christians set themselves between the Messiah and the Jews, hiding from the latter the authentic image of the Saviour" (cited in Doukhan, *Drinking at the Sources,* p. 93).

Even the well-known Protestant Reformer Martin Luther, who did not always say charitable things about the Jews, was compelled to crudely say the following about the Christians' beliefs and conduct: "Had I been a Jew I would have preferred to become a pig rather than a Christian, considering how those blockheads and jackasses govern and teach the Christian faith" (ibid., p. 97). Should the emphasis always be focused on Jewish conversion? Shouldn't the emphasis also be focused on real conversion and transformation for the many so-called Christians? The Jews would definitely respond more positively to our witness if we ourselves were truly converted and transformed, reflecting Christ's love and character in our lives. That is why the burden should not be solely placed on the Jews: "How come they don't accept Christ?" But the responsibility ought to be placed on us too: "What are we doing to make it easier for them to consider Christ?"

One of the possible reasons why the Jews emphasize their political entity in the Holy Land is that they think of it as a refuge of escape from the many centuries of prejudice and persecution at the hands of Christians. They place their emphasis on the land, not on the Lord, because He has been represented to them in a negative light. The land, the state of Israel, is what they cling to for their fulfillment as a people.

However, the kind of restoration that God intended for them, especially after the first advent of Jesus, was a spiritual restoration and not a physical one. He intended that their real restoration to Him be through accepting His Son as the Messiah. As we have observed earlier, this spiritual restoration was the passionate emphasis of Jesus and His apostles. In carefully studying the Bible, we find no hint whatsoever that the restoration would be a secular one.

The Old Testament emphasizes the conditional and moral prerequisites for the nation of Israel to continue to be God's special agent to the world. Such special status was given to Israel to share God's saving knowledge with the rest of humanity, and it was to exist *only* for the fulfillment of such purpose. Such a land was given to them for the purpose of being a blessing and a witness to the nations around them. What would happen to the land if they failed to meet that condition and ceased to be a witness to the world?

After spending hundreds of years waiting for the nation of Israel to accomplish His purposes, God gave the special responsibility of spreading the gospel to spiritual Israel, irrespective of race, nationality, or *geography*. God was not interested in a piece of real estate just for its own sake. Rather, He led the people Israel to that strategically and geographically central location so they would have easy access to all people around them in order to share His saving truth.

God allowed them to continue as a special nation and keep the land on the condition that they love and obey Him. Otherwise, what would be the difference between them and the other nations? God made it clear that the covenant included important conditions, for no covenant can stand without some stipulations.

As God made a covenant with them at Sinai, He clearly told them through Moses that " 'if you will indeed obey My voice and keep My covenant, then you shall be a special treasure to Me above all people. . . . And you shall be to Me a kingdom of priests and a holy nation' " (Exodus 19:5, 6). The same conditions for keeping the land applied not only to them but to the nations they replaced. God admonished them to stay faithful to Him, "lest the land vomit you out also when you defile it, as it vomited out the nations that were before you" (Leviticus 18:28).

In his book *The Moral Purpose of Prophecy*, Louis F. Were explains that the Jews were rigid literalists, like some modern theologians today. And that was one reason for their spiritual blindness and misunderstanding of their spiritual role and responsibility in the world. He writes: "The Jews were led to reject Christ because of their misinterpretation of the prophecies concerning Israel: They forgot or overlooked the moral purpose of prophecy—personal salvation from sin. . . . Spiritual pride, selfishness and sin in their hearts beclouded their spiritual discernment" (p. 19).

Today, some Christians make literal and rigid interpretation of promises and prophecies relating to Israel, and seem to clearly disregard these moral conditions. Because God was initially willing to accomplish His purposes through the nation of Israel, they believe He is strictly bound to that, regardless of how the nation of Israel acted, acts, or will act. But this is totally unbiblical. For "the total picture of the Old Testament eschatological remnant reveals that Israel's covenant blessings as a whole will be fulfilled, *not* in unbelieving national Israel, but only in that Israel which is faithful to Yahweh and trusts in His Messiah" (LaRondelle, *The Israel of God in Prophecy,* pp. 90, 91).

When the Old Testament is viewed as a unit, its main focus is clearly Messiah-centered. Everything in it converges on that center and finds meaning in its relation to it. If it seems to focus on Israel, it is only on believing Israel and what the Messiah will do through her in bringing salvation to the world. Those who do not discern the centeredness of the Messiah in the prophecies relating to Israel are spiritually blind. Jesus Himself told the Jewish leaders to "search the Scriptures, for in them you think you have eternal life; and these are they *which testify of Me*" (John 5:39, emphasis supplied). Those self-centered Jewish leaders, "having rejected Christ in His word, they rejected Him in person" (*The Desire of Ages,* p. 212).

Then after His resurrection, Jesus helped the two perplexed disciples on their way to Emmaus to understand and interpret the prophecies in a Christ-centered way. "Beginning at Moses and *all* the Prophets, He expounded to them in *all* the Scriptures the things concerning *Himself*" (Luke 24:27, emphasis supplied).

Many today are like those two disciples, perplexed about the prophecies relating to the Messiah and Israel. They must heed Christ's example by placing Him at the heart and center of Israel's historic calling as well as her prophetic mission. Paul confirms this fact by saying that indeed "*all* the promises of God *in Him* [Jesus] are *Yes*" (2 Corinthians 1:20, emphasis supplied).

The only way to properly understand the promises and prophecies is to find their Yes of emphasis and fulfillment in Christ. This is the only safe way to avoid the pitfalls of the many erroneous teachings today concerning this crucial subject. "In every page, whether history, or precept, or prophecy, the Old Testament Scriptures are irradiated with the glory of the Son of God. So far as it was of divine institution, the entire system of Judaism was a compacted prophecy of the gospel" (*The Desire of Ages*, p. 211).

This Christ-centered understanding of the Scriptures also renders invalid the literal Palestinian-centered system of interpretation. This belongs to the *futurist* school of prophetic interpretation, popularized by Hal Lindsey's book *The Late Great Planet Earth*. Futurism, as it is also referred to, focuses, among other things, on a future fulfillment of prophecies; the secret rapture; the literal restoration of Israel in Palestine; the rebuilding of the Jewish temple in Jerusalem, where the old sacrifices would be reinstated; and the mass conversion of the Jews at the beginning of the millennium.

By lifting passages out of their proper contexts, literal futurists destroy the unity and interrelatedness of God's plan of salvation with its prominent common thread throughout the Scriptures. Consequently, they develop different dispensations during which God treats people differently in relationship to their salvation. They believe God has dealt and will deal differently with Israel's salvation than with spiritual Israel.

The Jews are arbitrarily separated from the rest of humanity, to be given a special treatment and salvation by God. But such views, as we have seen in previous chapters, are diametrically opposed to the teachings of the prophets, Jesus, and the apostles. For example, the seventy-week (490 years) prophecy of Daniel is a continuous unit of time (as time logically is), allotted for literal Israel and ending in A.D. 34.

But the futurists came up with what is referred to as the "gap theory," which postpones the last seven years of that unbroken time period till the end of the Christian dispensation near the end of the world. They teach that, during that seven-year period, Christ will rapture the church, thus turning His full attention to the Jews. He will then supposedly work with them in the land of Palestine.

But let us be reasonable. How can they possibly treat time units that way? Time is naturally continuous and unbroken, and there exist no "gaps" in it. How can anyone, for example, postpone seven years of his life to some more convenient time in the future? Many people in our society who place great emphasis on "perpetual" youth and shun the aging process might not mind postponing a segment of their lives!

According to Hal Lindsey, the rapture of the saints will begin the seven-year period, which will culminate at the battle of Armageddon. At the commencement of these seven years, while the raptured saints are safely shielded in heaven from the terrible tribulation on earth, Jesus is going to appear in a special way to the Jews living in Israel. That will finally result in their acceptance of Him as the Messiah. Then He will commission 144,000 mighty Jewish evangelists, who will go throughout the world and convert more people than at any other time in history (see *The Late Great Planet Earth*, pp. 99, 100).

While this gigantic evangelistic endeavor is taking place, evil forces will be threatened by this great advance of the gospel and try to put a stop to it. At that time, a Roman antichrist dictator, rising out of a confederated European Common Market, will curiously come to the help of converted Israel and sign a cooperation treaty with it. This timely assistance will enable these Jews to rebuild the temple in Jerusalem during the first half of the seven years, at the spot where the Muslim Mosque stands.

But as they begin to offer sacrifices in the newly built temple, the antichrist will suddenly default on this treaty with the Jews and interrupt the temple services. And this will plunge the world into a horrible three and a half years (second half of the seven years) of tribulation, incited by the antichrist's cruel dictatorship. Toward the end of the seven years, a great Arab-African army will attack Israel, followed by a sudden attack by the Soviets, which gives them full control of the Middle East.

The antichrist hastily responds to this latest Soviet challenge to his authority by organizing a great army from Europe, joined by the

People's Republic of China, and possibly the United States. This gigantic army will destroy the Soviet occupation of Israel, along with the Arab-African army. This leaves the world in the grip of two remaining superpowers: the antichrist and his forces, and the powers of the Orient.

Now we finally come to the climax of Lindsey's fantastic scenario. These two remaining powers will fight the battle of Armageddon on the Plain of Megiddo in Israel for the ultimate control of the world. In the thick of this great war, Christ will appear with the saints, whom He had raptured seven years earlier, to destroy all the wicked and establish His kingdom there, and to rule the world from Jerusalem (see Lindsey for more details, particularly p. 151).

This makes a sensational scenario, and many Christians are intrigued by it and wholeheartedly believe it. Such a theory does not harmonize with the total message of the Bible and confuses many people. Now is the time for the Jews to believe in the Messiah and join spiritual Israel in evangelizing the world. Our preoccupation should not be with rebuilding an earthly temple or offering animal sacrifices, while Christ our substitutionary Sacrifice and High Priest mediates for us in the heavenly sanctuary. Rather, we should look for the heavenly city and for the glorious kingdom of Christ.

The great battle of Armageddon is a spiritual one between Christ, who will fight in behalf of His faithful remnant, and the evil forces under the leadership of Satan. It is also a battle for the minds and hearts of people, a battle for people's allegiance and loyalty to Christ or Satan. C. Mervyn Maxwell rhetorically comments: "Is it possible then that we should regard Armageddon not as a specific place (there being no such place!) but as being instead a symbolic *reminder* that in earth's final rebellion against truth and right, the God of truth and right will utterly *destroy His enemies* and totally *protect and preserve His people*?" (*God Cares,* vol. 2, p. 439, emphasis supplied).

Maxwell concludes that the battle of Armageddon "will not be

World War III. Nor will it be a military engagement on a cramped battlefield near the Mediterranean coast, fought in the hope of winning oil and Dead Sea minerals. And *neither will it be a battle confined in any special sense to the Middle East.* Remember: Neither 'valley of Jehoshaphat,' nor 'river Euphrates,' nor 'Babylon,' nor 'Armageddon' itself offers us any localized geographical significance." Maxwell asserts that this battle "will be a worldwide conflict pitting rebellious man and evil spirits against the Creator and His loyal followers. The outcome will be the eternal deliverance of God's people" (ibid., pp. 442, 443).

And while we are discussing Armageddon and futurism, we should mention the other two schools of prophetic interpretations. The *preterist* school, or preterism, sees the events referred to in the prophecies as lying in the past. Finally, the *historicist* school, or historicism, applies the various prophecies to past, present, and future events in history. The balanced view of historicism does not limit our understanding of prophecies to either the past, the present, or the future, but takes in the whole sweep of history. Such understanding allows us the freedom to place such fulfillments wherever they may properly fit in the successive phases of history.

Some similarities then, quite possibly exist between the ancient Jews and present futurists relating to the prophecies about the Messiah and Israel. Because of their literalistic and nationalist interpretation, the Jews missed out on the spiritual fulfillment relating to the suffering Messiah and spiritual Israel. Their obsession with their own views of expecting a political and temporal fulfillment made them ignore the realm of the spiritual.

Similarly, literal futurists of today are, to a certain degree, repeating the same tragic mistake of ancient Israel. They are so caught up in their emphasis on literal Jews and the modern state of Israel that they are undermining the spiritual fulfillment evident in the Christian church now, and the heavenly Canaan later.

Louis Were writes that "many futurists employ a system of types and antitypes but, because they believe things of *Israel* still belong to the *literal* Jews, they misapply the *antitypes*, in connection with *literal* Israel *in Palestine.*" Were goes on to amplify his explanation, asserting that "since Christ was enthroned in the heavenly temple and the Holy Spirit became His representative on earth, the types do *not have any literal, Palestinian* meaning: they are *spiritual* and *world-wide* in their *antitypical* applications" (*The Certainty of the Third Angel's Message*, p. 45, emphasis supplied).

The political and spiritual situation in Israel today does not show in any way that the Jews are the restored people of God. What conditions have they met? Have they returned to God with all their hearts and accepted His offer of salvation through Jesus Christ? Are they witnessing to others about their faith in Christ? Unfortunately not. So how could their establishment of the state of Israel be God's reward for their faithfulness to Him? What has spiritually changed since Jesus said to them, "The Kingdom of God will be taken from you and given to a nation bearing the fruits of it" (Matthew 21:43)?

Someone may ask, why then are they established in Israel as a nation after almost 2,000 years of dispersion? That question fascinates may people and unfortunately leads them to hastily conclude that their reestablishment is the result of the literal fulfillments of biblical prophecies. But even if the Jews were to accept Christ as the Messiah and turn to Him wholeheartedly, that would have nothing to do with their political status or physical restoration. Since the Jews rejected His Son, God is no longer using a single race or nation to spread the gospel to all the world but is using the universal remnant of spiritual Israel.

Therefore, the existence of the modern state of Israel cannot be a sign of God's favor to the unbelieving Jews living there. Though they justify their presence there by citing political, military, or international reasons, they cannot base their claim on the fulfillment of biblical promises or prophecies. Though they live in the heart of Israel, unless their hearts are turned toward Christ, they are working against Him, and their presence there does not have any spiritual significance.

It's futile to think that a relationship exists between the modern state of Israel and biblical prophecies. Such prophecies have no relevance to what is happening in the Middle East now or what will happen there in the future. For God is no longer dealing with any particular nation, and His promises belong now to the church, the "Israel of God." Frank Holbrook asserts in this connection that "any Jewish government that arises after that [A.D. 34] is a purely secular one. It would develop only in the same way that any other political power would rise" (*The Enigma of Israel,* p. 47).

Of course, one can sympathize with the Jewish desire for freedom and security, as we must do for all peoples living in the Middle East or any other part of the world. However, one shouldn't twist the Scriptures, giving unwarranted interpretations to unduly support his sentiment or zealousness of Israel. The Palestinians, too, need to enjoy freedom, security, and the Saviour's message of salvation as much as any people. As Christians, our emphasis ought to be focused on the promised Lord and not so much focused on the Promised Land.

Our emphasis should not be political but spiritual. Our mission is to reach out with love, justice, and impartiality to all the descendants of Abraham, be they Jews or Muslims. Our commission is to take the gospel of Christ to all people, Jews and Gentiles, and any others. And in doing that we trust that those who believe in Him will join the believing remnant in helping to finish the task of spreading the gospel and hastening Christ's return.

The time will soon come when Christ shall suddenly return to this old world, put an end to *all* its kingdoms, and establish *His* everlasting kingdom. Therefore, our thoughts and hopes ought to be on that imperishable kingdom and not on our earthly kingdoms, which will soon be swept away as the chaff of the field. The time is ripe for the stone cut out of the mountain without human hands, which represents Christ, to hurl itself upon all the nations in the final judgment. This stone "shall break in pieces and consume all these kingdoms, and it shall stand forever" (Daniel 2:44).

Upon pronouncing His judgment on the unfruitful nation of Israel, in Matthew 21:42-44, Jesus applied to Himself the Messianic prophecy of the rejected chief cornerstone found in Psalm 118:22, 23. Also, the apostle Paul explains that this chief cornerstone became a stumbling stone and a rock of offense to the Jews (see Romans 9:32, 33; see also 1 Peter 2:4-8). Jesus said to the unfaithful Jewish leaders, who took offense in Him, "whoever falls on this stone will be broken; but on whomever it falls, it will grind him to powder" (Matthew 21:44).

What does it mean to fall on the Rock and be broken? It "is to give up our self-righteousness and to go to Christ with the humility of a child, repenting of our transgressions, and believing in His forgiving love" (*The Desire of Ages*, p. 599). With this contriteness of heart, we may be broken on the Rock, but not crushed by it. That is our only security and assurance of salvation. Being anchored in Jesus, the living Stone, transforms us into the living stones of His kingdom and makes us one with His eternal kingdom, which will soon become a great mountain and fill the whole earth.

In patience and mercy, Christ the living Stone is still pleading with all—Jews, Muslims, Gentiles, or whomever—to come and be established in Him. We must become established in Him before He descends to this earth as the Stone of judgment. Now this Stone is "broad enough for *all*, and strong enough to sustain the weight and burden of the whole world" (ibid.).

We are living at the very end of history, long after the kingdoms represented by the toes of the statue in Daniel's prophecy (see Daniel 2:33, 34). There is only one kingdom left to emerge on the world's cosmic scene, and that is the eternal kingdom of the King of kings. It is crucial for us to focus our thoughts and our hopes on what is eternal and heavenly, and not on what is temporal and earthly.

But we still live in this sinful world. And we see how the modern descendants of Abraham bitterly fight for every inch of land they can grasp. What a far cry from the example of their father Abraham!

He did not even possess a burial place for his beloved wife Sarah. And when there was a contention about the grazing land for his flocks and the flocks of his nephew Lot, he was reasonable and accommodating. At the risk of sounding pessimistic, a real solution will never be found for the long turmoil among the present-day descendants of Abraham (and all peoples, for that matter) without following the example of Abraham.

Abraham experienced a genuine faith in God. He experienced true and close friendship with God, born out of his abiding trust in Him. His focus was not on his will, but on God's will; not on his own righteousness, but on God's saving righteousness manifested in the sacrifice of His Son Jesus; not on a passing reward, but on the eternal one. As a sojourner, he was not attached to the perishable things of this world, but to Christ, whose day he saw and was glad.

Our father Abraham knew that in this world "we have no continuing city, but we seek the one to come." So as the faithful seed of our father Abraham, let us, like him, wait for "the city which has foundations, whose builder and maker is God." And let us go with him to "Mount Zion and to the city of the living God, the heavenly Jerusalem, to an innumerable company of angels" (Hebrews 13:14; 11:10; 12:22).

Bibliography

Books

Anderson, Rey Allen, and Jay Milton Hoffman. *All Eyes on Israel.* Fort Worth, Tex.: Harvest Press, Inc., 1976.

Carmody, Denise Lardner, and John Tully Carmody. *Ways to the Center.* Belmont, Calif.: Wadsorth Publishing Company, 1989.

Carter, Jimmy. *The Blood of Abraham.* Boston, Mass.: Houghton, Mifflin & Company, 1985.

Damsteegt, Gerard P. *Foundations of the SDA Message and Mission.* Grand Rapids, Mich.: Wm. B. Eerdmans Pub. Co., 1977.

Doukhan, Jacques. *Drinking at the Sources.* Boise, Idaho: Pacific Press Publishing Association, 1981.

Epstein, Isidore. *Judaism.* Baltimore, Md.: Penguin Books, 1974.

Friedman, Thomas L. *From Beirut to Jerusalem.* New York, N.Y.: Farrar Strauss Giroux, 1989.

Fry, C. George, and James R. King. *Islam: A Survey of the Muslim Faith.* Grand Rapids, Mich.: Baker Book House, 1980.

Furness, Jim. *Vital Words of the Bible.* Grand Rapids, Mich.: Wm. B. Eerdmans Pub. Co., 1966.

Gartenhaus, Jacob. *Unto His Own.* London, England: C. Tinung & Company, 1965.

Gilbert, F. C. *Practical Lessons.* Nashville, Tenn.: Southern Publishing Association, 1972.

Hasel, Gerhard F. *The Remnant.* Berrien Springs, Mich.: Andrews University Press, 1972.

———. "The Song of the Vineyard," North American Bible Conferences, 1974. Prepared by the General Conference of Seventh-day Adventists Biblical Research Committee.

Heschel, Abraham. *Between God and Man.* New York, N.Y.: Harper & Row, 1959.

Hitti, Philip K. *The Arabs.* Chicago, Ill.: Henry Regnesy Company, 1967.

Holbrook, Frank B. *The Enigma of Israel.* Nashville, Tenn.: Southern

Publishing Association, 1975.

Horn, Siegfried. *The Spade Confirms the Book.* Washington, D.C.: Review and Herald Publishing Association, 1980.

Lapide, Pinchas, and Ulrich Luz. *Jesus in Two Perspectives.* Minneapolis, Minn.: Augsburg Publishing House, 1985.

LaRondelle, Hans K. *Chariots of Salvation.* Hagerstown, Md.: Review and Herald Publishing Association, 1987.

———. *The Israel of God in Prophecy.* Berrien Springs, Mich.: Andrews University Press, 1983.

Lilienthal, Alfred M. *The Zionist Connection II.* New York, N.Y.: Dodd, Mead & Company, 1978.

Lindsey, Hal. *The Late Great Planet Earth.* Grand Rapids, Mich.: Zondervan, 1972.

Ludwig, Theodore M. *The Sacred Paths: Understanding the Religions of the World.* New York, N.Y.: Macmillan Publishing Company, 1989.

Maxwell, C. Mervyn. *God Cares.* Vol. 1, *The Message of Daniel.* Boise, Idaho: Pacific Press Publishing Association, 1981.

———. *God Cares.* Vol. 2, *The Message of Revelation.* Boise, Idaho: Pacific Press Publishing Association, 1981.

Noss, David S., and John B. Noss. *A History of the World's Religions,* 8th edition. New York, N.Y.: Macmillan Publishing Company, 1990.

Oesterreicher, John M., editor. *The Bridge—A Yearbook of Judeo-Christian Studies.* Vol. 1. New York, N.Y.: Pantheon Books, 1955.

Oster, Kenneth. *Islam Reconsidered.* Hicksville, N.Y.: Exposition Press, 1979.

Rahman, Fazlur. *Islam.* Garden City, N.Y.: Doubleday & Company, Inc., 1966.

Renckens, Henry. *The Religion of Israel.* New York, N.Y.: Sheed and Ward, 1966.

Rice, Richard. *The Reign of God.* Berrien Springs, Mich.: Andrews University Press, 1985.

Rosten, Leo. *Religions of America.* New York, N.Y.: Simon & Schuster, Inc., 1975.

Sadat, Jehan. *A Woman of Egypt.* New York, N.Y.: Simon & Schuster, 1987.

Samaan, Philip G. *Portraits of the Messiah.* Hagerstown, Md.: Review and Herald Publishing Association, 1989.

Sandmel, Samuel. *The Several Israels.* New York, N.Y.: Ktav Publishing

House, Inc., 1971.

Seamands, John T. *Tell It Well.* Kansas City, Mo.: Beacon Hill Press, 1981.

Seventh-day Adventists Answer Questions on Doctrines, prepared by a representative group of SDA leaders, Bible teachers and editors. Washington, D.C.: Review and Herald Publishing Association, 1957.

Seventh-day Adventists Believe . . . A Biblical Exposition of 27 Fundamental Doctrines. Ministerial Association, General Conference of SDA. Hagerstown, Md.: Review and Herald Publishing Association, 1988.

Shorrosh, Anis. A. *Islam Revealed—A Christian Arab's View of Islam.* Nashville, Tenn.: Thomas Nelson Publishers, 1988.

Starkes, M. Thomas. *Islam and Eastern Religions.* Nashville, Tenn.: Convention Press, 1981.

Toynbee, Arnold. *Civilization on Trial.* New York, N.Y.: Oxford University Press, 1948.

Twain, Mark. *The Adventures of Huckleberry Finn.* New York, N.Y.: Regents Publishing Company, 1954.

Vandeman, George E. *Decade of Destiny.* Boise, Idaho: Pacific Press Publishing Association, 1989.

———. *Showdown at Armageddon.* Boise, Idaho: Pacific Press Publishing Association, 1987.

Venden, Morris L. *Uncommon Ground.* Boise, Idaho: Pacific Press Publishing Association, 1984.

Were, Louis F. *The Certainty of the Third Angel's Message.* Berrien Springs, Mich.: First Impressions, 1981.

———. *The Moral Purpose of Prophecy.* Berrien Springs, Mich.: First Impressions, 1989.

White, Ellen G. *The Acts of the Apostles.* Boise, Idaho: Pacific Press Publishing Association, 1911.

———. *Christ's Object Lessons.* Pacific Press, 1941.

———. *The Desire of Ages.* Pacific Press, 1940.

———. *Education.* Pacific Press, 1952.

———. *Evangelism.* Washington, D.C.: Review and Herald Publishing Association, 1946.

———. *The Great Controversy.* Pacific Press, 1950.

———. Letter 42, 1912.

———. *The Ministry of Healing.* Pacific Press, 1942.

———. *Patriarchs and Prophets.* Pacific Press, 1913.

———. *Prophets and Kings.* Pacific Press, 1943.

———. *Sketches From the Life of Paul.* Washington, D.C.: Review and Herald Publishing Association, 1974.

———. *Steps to Christ.* Pacific Press, 1956.

———. "The Need of Home Religion." *Review and Herald,* June 29, 1905.

———. *Thoughts From the Mount of Blessing.* Pacific Press, 1956.

———. *What Ellen G. White Says About Work for the Jewish People.* Prepared by North American Mission Committee, General Conference of SDA, revised 1976.

Wieland, Robert J. *In Search of the Treasure Faith.* Accra, Ghana: All Africa Publications, 1986.

Wilson, John F., and Royce W. Clark. *Religion: A Preface.* Englewood Cliffs, N.J.: Prentice Hall, 1989.

Yates, Kyle M., ed. *The Religious World.* New York, N.Y.: Macmillan Publishing Company, 1988.

Articles

Bernstein, Carl. "The Agony Over Israel." *Time,* May 7, 1990.

Cryderman, Lyn. "Who Is a Jew?" *Christianity Today,* February 5, 1990.

Duffy, Brian, Louise Lief, et al. "The World's Most Dangerous Man." *U.S. News & World Report,* June 4, 1990.

Gladson, Jerry. "Israel's Failure to Fulfill God's Purpose." *Review and Herald,* November 4, 1976.

"Global Mission," *Adventist Review,* July 5, 1990.

Johnsson, William. "Killing for God's Sake." *Liberty,* May-June 1983.

Lane, Charles. "A Time Bomb at the City's Heart." *Newsweek,* October 22, 1990.

LaRondelle, Hans. "One Saviour—One People." Unpublished Manuscript, July 1990.

Lawton, Kim A. "An Elusive Peace." *Christianity Today,* April 21, 1989.

Mathews, Tom, Rod Nordland, and Carroll Bogert. "The Long Shadow," *Newsweek,* May 7, 1990.

Shea, William. "Leaving Egypt." *Adventist Review,* May 17, 1990.

Specht, Walter. "New Testament Israel." *Adventist Review,* November 11, 1976.

Watts, Kit. "A String of Surprises." *Adventist Review,* June 14, 1990.

Wong, Pamela Pearson. "Document Angers Jewish Community." *Christianity Today,* September 22, 1989.

Bible Commentaries and Dictionaries

Barnes, Albert. *Barnes' Notes on the Old and New Testaments: Luke and John.* Grand Rapids, Mich.: Baker Book House, 1980.

Barrett, C. K. *Harper's N.T. Commentaries: The Epistle to the Romans.* New York: Harper & Row Publishers, 1957.

Clarke, Adam. *Clarke's Commentary,* vols. 1 and 2. Nashville, Tenn.: Abingdon Press.

Keil, C. F., and F. Delitzsch. *Commentary on the Old Testament,* vol. 1. Grand Rapids, Mich.: Wm. B. Eerdmans Publishing Company, reprinted, 1973.

Laymon, Charles M., ed. *The Interpreter's One-Volume Commentary on the Bible.* Nashville, Tenn.: Abingdon Press, 1984.

Metzger, Bruce M., ed. *The Greek New Testament, Dictionary,* 2nd ed. Stuttgart, West Germany: Wurttemberg Bible Society, 1968.

Neufeld, Don F., ed. *Seventh-day Adventist Bible Dictionary,* revised edition. Hagerstown, Md.: Review and Herald Publishing Association, 1979.

Nichol, F. D., ed. *Seventh-day Adventist Bible Commentary,* vols. 1, 4, 6, 7. Washington, D.C.: Review and Herald Publishing Association, 1980.